MICROSOFT POWERPOINT MADE EASY

This is a FLAME TREE book
First published 2013

Publisher and Creative Director: Nick Wells
Project Editor: Polly Prior
Art Director and Layout Design: Mike Spender
Digital Design and Production: Chris Herbert
Technical Editor: Roger Laing
Copy Editor: Daniela Nava
Proofreader: Karen Fitzpatrick
Screenshots: Chris Smith
Thanks to: Laura Bulbeck and Lydia Good

This edition first published 2013 by
FLAME TREE PUBLISHING
Crabtree Hall, Crabtree Lane
Fulham, London SW6 6TY
United Kingdom

www.flametreepublishing.com

13 15 17 16 14
1 3 5 7 9 10 8 6 4 2

© 2013 Flame Tree Publishing Ltd

ISBN 978-0-85775-524-7

Printed in China

All non-screenshot pictures are courtesy of Shutterstock and © the following photographers:
Yuri Arcurs 4, 7, 12, 220; Tyler Boyes 74 b; Diego Cervo 3; r.classen 5 b, 86; JazzBoo 42 b; karam Miri 207;
Dmitriy Shironosov 1; .shock 5 t, 46; T.W. van Urk 6 b, 188; Angela Waye 6 t, 136

MICROSOFT
POWERPOINT®
MADE EASY

CHRIS SMITH

**FLAME TREE
PUBLISHING**

CONTENTS

If you're unfamiliar with Microsoft PowerPoint, things can get a little intimidating. Using easy-to-digest steps, this chapter introduces this versatile presentation software and furnishes you with the knowledge needed to feel comfortable. You'll learn what PowerPoint is capable of, what you can include in a slide show and take a detailed look at the PowerPoint Window and the user interface you'll be working with en route to PowerPoint nirvana.

CREATING A PRESENTATION

This chapter features a comprehensive guide to creating and delivering a basic PowerPoint presentation, with step-by-step instructions on how to start a new document, add text and insert new slides. It also introduces the vast array of attractive themes and templates that Microsoft has provided to enable you to brighten up your presentation. You'll also find vital information on preparing to deliver your presentation, transferring it to the big screen and printing handouts to allow your audience to follow and make notes of their own.

IMPROVING A PRESENTATION

PowerPoint features a gigantic array of options for improving the look and content of a presentation. This chapter offers a detailed guide to selecting, editing and spell-checking text, while also changing the fonts, colours and style of important words. There is also plenty of advice on how to improve the look of your slide show by adding attractive animations and transitions, and creating custom slide designs.

Now comes the fun part! This portion of the book focuses on adding meat to the bones of a PowerPoint presentation. The software allows you to add images, video and sound, as well as attractive charts, tables, shapes and SmartArt (fantastic text-based diagrams). The chapter features clear and easy-to-follow instructions for perfecting the more exciting portions of any PowerPoint document that'll keep your audience bright-eyed and bushy-tailed.

Are you ready to take things to the next level? This chapter focuses on advanced functionality like broadcasting your presentation on the web or turning your beautiful slide show into a video for the world to behold. It also illustrates how to share your presentation so colleagues can contribute, how to review changes to the document and how to create clickable slides with links to websites, other documents and more.

POWERPOINT PROJECTS 220

The final section of this book features a detailed step-by-step guide to creating fantastic PowerPoint presentations in a variety of settings: for business, for learning and for the home. Each project has been produced on either Mac or PC (although the same results can be achieved on either using the tools outlined within this book) and is accompanied by helpful screenshots so you'll see exactly how it's been done, and hopefully pick up plenty of useful tips along the way.

INTRODUCTION

Since its arrival on the scene in 1990, PowerPoint has developed into the world's most popular means of presenting computerized information to an audience. You'll see it in many settings: from the classroom and the office to your local pub or church. This book offers a practical and educational guide, which will quickly allow you to build up your skills while resolving the roadblocks you'll encounter on the way to producing great slide shows.

GETTING TO GRIPS WITH POWERPOINT

Although PowerPoint can appear to be quite intimidating and complex to the first-time or inexperienced user, everything is designed and laid out in a logical way, which makes it very easy to understand. This book will break down some of the boundaries and allow you to explore the full potential of the software; you'll be amazed at how straightforward everything is once the first slide is written.

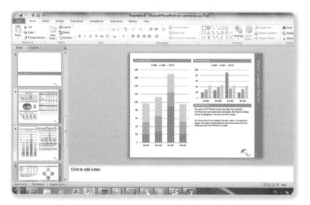

Above: PowerPoint may be intimidating to the first-time user, but it is laid out in a logical way, making it easy to use.

DIVE IN, DIVE OUT

This book is not meant to be read from cover to cover; frankly, we'd be worried about you if you did. It is our hope that you'll dive in and out whenever you need a helping hand to understand a particular feature or overcome a frustrating problem. If you need to learn how to add secondary paragraphs to bullet points, how to add a legend to a chart or how to make an image fit a placeholder, just look it up in the index page.

FORGET THE STIGMAS

Let's be honest: the word 'PowerPoint' doesn't really inspire positive connotations. Many of us will have sat through dull presentations, wishing to be elsewhere. However, it doesn't have to be that way; PowerPoint presentations can be as exciting, interesting and entertaining as you want to make them. All of the tools to do so are available at the click of a mouse and a few prods of the keyboard. This book will help you harness them and prove the naysayers wrong.

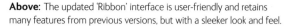

VERSIONS

PowerPoint is a constantly evolving platform, and each new version of the software brings changes and refinements. Features get upgraded, renamed, moved around or sometimes ditched altogether. All of this can occasionally confuse and frustrate users who are familiar with the earlier incarnations.

Above: The updated 'Ribbon' interface is user-friendly and retains many features from previous versions, but with a sleeker look and feel.

Microsoft completely overhauled the look and feel of PowerPoint (and the rest of the Office suite) in 2007, with a new user interface known as 'the Ribbon', which was a large departure from the earlier versions. This book is largely tailored towards the newer PowerPoint 2010 and PowerPoint 2007 versions, but large differences relating to older versions will be explained where appropriate.

Above: The differences between PowerPoint for Mac and Windows will be explored throughout the book.

APPLE MAC USERS

Apple computers are as popular as ever and, thankfully for those who prefer to work with the Mac operating system rather than

Windows, Microsoft makes a fully functional version of PowerPoint for both platforms. There are some subtle and not-so-subtle differences between the two pieces of software that will be explained in detail later on.

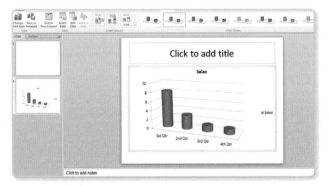

Above: Chapter four of this book focuses on tools and techniques to spice up your presentation, such as inserting a chart into a slide.

SIX CHAPTERS

This book is split into six chapters and, naturally, there's a logical progression from one to the next, depending on the skill level associated with each feature of PowerPoint. Chapter one gives a quick overview for those who may be new to PowerPoint. Chapter two equips you with all of the tools necessary to create and deliver the most basic presentation to an audience. Chapter three focuses on the improvements you can make through design and text formatting tools, while in Chapter four the focus is on spicing up your presentation with a range of attractive charts, tables, videos, images and more. With some advanced tips, Chapter five will enable you to go from Padawan learner to Jedi master, while the final chapter features step-by-step case studies you can apply to creating the perfect PowerPoint presentations for work, home and school.

HOT TIPS AND SHORTCUTS

Hoping to save you a little time, we've inserted throughout the book plenty of tips to help you access some of the neat, but less obvious features within PowerPoint. Speaking of time-savers, Microsoft has inserted a host of keyboard short cuts. These usually involve pressing two or more keys together (e.g. Control+N for a New Presentation) rather than using three or four different mouse clicks. Wherever these shortcuts are available, we'll point them out.

EASY DIGESTION

Sometimes the amount of information required to get to grips with a certain feature can be quite intimidating, so we've tried to break it down into manageable and easily digestible chunks. Rather than a gigantic Sunday roast piled on to your plate, which leaves you sluggish, demotivated and ready for a nap, think of this book as a relaxing evening picking and choosing from a tapas bar. Where necessary, we've also included a host of screenshots from the Mac and PC versions to further illustrate the features described throughout.

Above: This book is easy to dip in and out of and will guide you through all the tools you need for setting up a presentation.

BUSTING THE JARGON

Although every effort has been made to keep the language and tone as user-friendly as possible, sometimes using jargon like 'placeholder' and 'AutoCorrect' is unavoidable. That's just what the features are called! Whenever you see a term or word you're unfamiliar with, head to the Glossary of Terms for an explanation (or you could use the Thesaurus tool within PowerPoint).

HELP!

Although we're confident that this book provides all of the information needed to become fluent in the language of PowerPoint, Microsoft also includes a very useful 'Help' section within the software. Typing your query into the Help box will bring answers to any question you may have. This may be particularly useful if you're creating PowerPoint presentations in older versions of the software that haven't been explored in as much depth here. You can also check out the Further Reading section at the end of this book for a number of helpful websites.

POWERPOINT BASICS

WHAT IS POWERPOINT?

PowerPoint is a versatile piece of presentation software made by Microsoft primarily for use on desktop and laptop personal computers. These first few pages will help you to understand the very basics of what PowerPoint is, what it can do and how you can get it up and running on your computer.

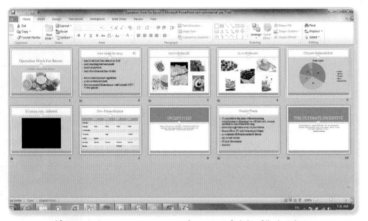

WHAT IS PRESENTATION SOFTWARE?

Presentation software – and, in our case, PowerPoint – is a modern combination of the traditional blackboard, whiteboard, flip chart, overhead projector slide and printed handout. It can substitute or complement any of those. A presentation

Above: A presentation consists of a series of slides filled with various pieces of information, like text, pictures, charts and videos.

consists of a series of computerized 'slides' filled with various pieces of information. The software requires a computer on which to create the presentation and a screen of some description in order to view it.

WHY USE POWERPOINT?

PowerPoint has become the most popular software for presenting and sharing information with an audience, whether you're at home, school or work. It can be used for the most basic text-based presentations or for meticulously designed shows, which include videos,

pictures, audio, charts, graphs and much, much more. Starting at the very beginning, we'll help you on the way to achieving both.

Do I Have It Already?

If you're coming to this book as a complete newcomer, you may be wondering how to go about obtaining PowerPoint and how to get it on to your computer.

Above: Click on the Start button on Windows to check if you have PowerPoint.

However, there's a chance you may already have it on your computer at work, school or home. If you have Microsoft Word on your computer then you probably have PowerPoint too (look for the software represented by the 'P' icon like Word's 'W' within the Microsoft Office package).

PowerPoint Within Microsoft Office

PowerPoint can be purchased on its own but forms a vital component of the Microsoft Office package (or 'suite', as it's generally known). It is much more cost-effective to buy the Office suite as a whole and we can safely predict that you'll get plenty of use from the other items within the suite. Here are some of the other popular Office programs you may recognize.

Hot Tip

To check if you have PowerPoint, hit the Start button at the bottom-left corner of Windows (Hit Command (⌘) + Space on Mac) and type 'PowerPoint' into the search box. If it appears in the pop-up menu then you're good to go.

Above: You may already have PowerPoint on your computer, especially if you have Microsoft Word.

- **Word**: The world's most popular word processor, it is used to create and edit text-based documents.

- **Excel**: Software used to create spreadsheets and analyse data.

- **OneNote**: Note-taking software often used for creating to-do lists and reminders.

- **Access**: A database tool for gathering important information, such as mailing lists, in one place.

- **Outlook**: Microsoft's de facto email client used for sending and receiving email.

PowerPoint on the Apple Mac

Since Microsoft makes PowerPoint, a common misunderstanding is that this software is only available on Windows-based PC computers. However, Mac users need not despair. PowerPoint is also available for Mac computers. The Mac version of the software is very similar to the PC version and boasts nearly all of the same features. However, there are many differences, which are usually related to the naming of these features and the means of accessing them through the various menus, toolbars and keyboard short cuts. This book will assist Mac users in equal measure as those using PCs and when differences arise, we will point them out. However, when differences are very slight, we'll rely on your common sense to spot them and act accordingly.

PowerPoint 2010 (PowerPoint 2011 for Mac)

This book will primarily focus on the latest and greatest version of the software, which is PowerPoint 2010 for PC and PowerPoint 2011 for Mac (generally speaking, the newer Mac versions are released a year after their Windows equivalents, but the feature sets are much the same).

Older Versions

PowerPoint has been around in various forms for over 25 years and has constantly been updated, redesigned and improved in that time. Traditionally, Microsoft brings out at least one new version of the software each time it updates the Windows operating system (OS); for example, PowerPoint 2010 was designed to work with Windows 7. It's highly unlikely that you'll be using a version beyond those listed below and if you are, it's time to upgrade!

Above: This book focuses on the latest versions of PowerPoint, but we'll discuss older versions throughout too.

⊝ PowerPoint 2007 for Windows (PowerPoint 2008 for Mac): The second most recent version, which was launched alongside the now uncommon and unpopular Windows Vista OS

⊝ PowerPoint 2003 for Windows (PowerPoint 2004 for Mac): Built for use on the existing Microsoft Windows XP OS, it offered improvements on PowerPoint XP.

⊝ PowerPoint XP/2002 was launched alongside the Windows XP OS in 2001.

Changes to PowerPoint 2010

PowerPoint 2010 for PC was more of an evolutionary version of the software, building on the revolution of PowerPoint 2007, which brought the complete change in design and user interface. If you're coming to PowerPoint 2010 from 2007, you'll perceive very little difference between the two programs, whereas if you're familiar with PowerPoint 2003 and coming to 2010 or 2007 then you'll notice a huge difference.

Since PowerPoint 2007, the means of finding your way around now centres on the Ribbon tabs (*see* page 33), which have replaced some of the traditional menus and toolbars that appeared at the very top of the screen within PowerPoint 2003 and earlier versions.

Other PowerPoint 2010 features that weren't present in previous versions are listed below and they will be explained in much greater detail throughout the book.

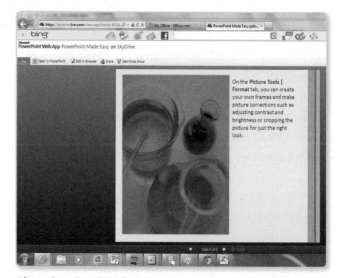

Above: PowerPoint 2010 features that weren't present in previous versions, such as using PowerPoint online, will be looked at later in the book.

- **Backstage View**: A new way to manage your PowerPoint presentation files (*see page 36*).

- **Save to the web**: Upload your presentation to an online storage locker.

- **Collaboration**: Working together with colleagues on one presentation.

- **Save versions**: Ensuring you don't lose older versions of presentations.

- **Sections**: Easily breaking down large presentations into smaller pieces.

- **Web apps**: Work from anywhere by using PowerPoint online.

Using This Book with Older Versions of PowerPoint

This book is largely based around the tools within PowerPoint 2010 for PC and PowerPoint 2011 for Mac, but if you're working with 2007 or 2003 it'll still be helpful, as a large proportion of the functionality within 2010 is available in the earlier versions – just accessible in different ways. In order to save explaining everything multiple times, here are the simple rules you need to remember:

⊖ PowerPoint 2007 and 2010 are extremely similar aside from the new features listed previously; access to nearly all features will be the same.

⊖ There's no Backstage View in 2007 and 2003. Most of the same functionality will appear within the Office Button (2007) and File Menu (2003), but there are variations.

⊖ Most things that are accessible in the Ribbon in 2007/2010 will appear within the menus in 2003. So instead of finding Save in the File tab, you'll find it in the File menu, and instead of hitting the Slide Show tab you will need to hit the Slide Show menu to play your slide show.

Above: Most things that are accessible in the Ribbon in 2007/2010 will appear within the menus in 2003.

Future Versions of PowerPoint

As Microsoft's Windows operating system evolves and improves, so does Microsoft Office and PowerPoint. PowerPoint 2013 will launch in late 2012 or early 2013. Among the new features, PowerPoint 2013 adds a new and improved landing page when the software is opened, new colour themes for templates, an improved Presenter View, easier ways to embed online videos from various sources, multiple user interface changes and enhanced collaboration tools. PowerPoint 2013 will not be available for Mac users, but Microsoft is likely to update PowerPoint 2011 with a new version sometime in 2013 or 2014.

Hot Tip

Where differences are prevalent enough to point out, look out for 'Older Versions' boxes. As the minute details of using those features will not be present, use the Help menu in PowerPoint.

WHAT CAN I DO WITH POWERPOINT?

Since the possibilities are endless, a more fitting question might be: 'What can't I do with PowerPoint?' You can build a college presentation, family slide show, business pitch, fitness plan, karaoke lyric sheet, an interactive information station and even a question slide show for the local pub quiz. You may be familiar with some of the uses we'll highlight, but others may surprise you.

WHERE POWERPOINT IS USED

Unless you're a newcomer to planet Earth, you will probably have been exposed to a PowerPoint presentation in one or more of their many forms.

In the Office

The occasional misuse or overuse of PowerPoint in the workplace has earned it a reputation as an effective cure for insomnia, but it really doesn't have to be that way. With a little help from these pages, you'll be able to pull off the following with engaging panache.

- **Sales reports:** For more perspective on improved figures, you can create a presentation loaded with attractive visual charts.

- **Pitching an idea:** If you've had a brainwave then a slide show can better illustrate your 'Eureka!' moment.

- **Training employees:** PowerPoint shows can help newcomers to settle in while learning more about their new position and company.

Job interview: As application rates continue to rise, everyone's looking for an edge and a head-turning slideshow could be yours.

In the Classroom

This software has been a time-saving godsend for both teachers and students looking for an interesting way to present their lectures and work.

Lectures: Accompanied by a printed handout (*see page 70*) on which students can make their own notes, these presentations are a great way to deliver information in easy-to-digest portions.

Homework/Coursework: PowerPoint makes it easy to remember your key talking points, while helping you to move at a lively pace that keeps things interesting for your classmates and tutors.

At Home

A PowerPoint presentation in the home can be a great tool to rally the troops for a trip or to present special memories.

Above: With a little help from these pages, you'll be able to pull off using PowerPoint in the office with panache.

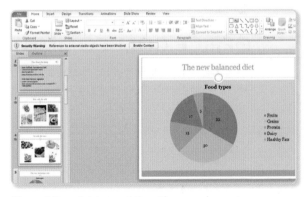

Above: A PowerPoint presentation at home can be great for sharing special memories, or organizing a trip with the help of maps and videos.

Photo albums: PowerPoint features a number of tools for easily crafting annotated photo albums complete with video, a soundtrack and more.

⊖ **Planning a trip**: If you're exploring the great outdoors, you can pack a presentation with maps, videos and information about your destination.

⊖ **Family budgeting/dieting**: Time for a bit of belt tightening (literally and figuratively) at home? Here's how you sell it to the rest of the clan.

Beyond the Holy Trinity

This versatile software can also be put to good use in other situations.

⊖ **Information posts**: Museums and galleries are using PowerPoint to create interactive stations where visitors can learn more about exhibits, watch video, listen to audio or answer trivia.

⊖ **Lyrics sheets**: If you co-ordinate a choir or are responsible for furnishing your parishioners with hymn lyrics, you can easily create and project song sheets.

OFFICE.COM COMMUNITY TEMPLATES

We'll explain templates in greater detail within Chapter two (*see* page 53) but their presence merits a mention here, as easily accessible, user designed templates enable us to use PowerPoint in a number of less familiar ways.

Above: Office.com templates offer a number of less familiar PowerPoint uses such as for a CV, invitation, calendar or family tree.

⊖ **CV**: Give your résumé a well-earned refresh.

⊖ **Birthday invitation**: Create an invitation which would make your five year-old proud.

⊖ **Calendar**: Easy-to-edit calendars, and attractive financial and academic year planners.

⊖ **Family Tree**: Charting and presenting your family history.

⊖ **Labels**: Ideal for large gatherings.

THE ROAD TO A SUCCESSFUL POWERPOINT SHOW

In order to whet your appetite for what lies ahead, we thought of a way to compare a PowerPoint presentation to a delicious meal. A Hamburger (or in our case, text) is always nice, but it's always better if you add cheese (pictures), bacon (video), mushrooms (pie charts) and grilled onions (audio).

SLIDES

Within a PowerPoint presentation, the different pages are called 'slides'. To continue with our hamburger analogy, slides are the bread rolls on which to place all of those yummy fillings: the text, audio, video, etc. As you move from slide to slide, your presentation will progress in much the same way that an old-fashioned carousel slide projector moves through photographs.

Within PowerPoint there's an array of slide designs you can choose from to suit your presentation, and once you've mastered the basics, you can get fancy and take a stab at designing your own.

Text

The easiest way to get started with PowerPoint is to create a presentation filled only with words, which is where Chapter

> **Hot Tip**
>
> **Keep it simple. Depending on your purposes, simply adding text is enough to create an adequate presentation ... but where's the fun in that?**

two (*see* page 48) comes in handy. You can type directly into a pre-made text box called a content placeholder (*see* page 60) using your PC's or laptop's keyboard, just as you would if you were writing a Microsoft Word document. However, bullet points or lists are often used in presentations to introduce talking points that are then explained more in-depth.

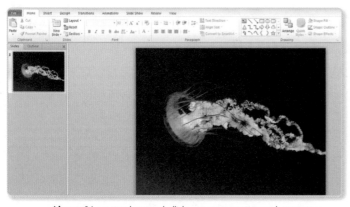

Above: It's so simple to embellish your presentation with your own photos or striking images from the internet!

Above: It's simple to add videos to your show that you've shot using your camera or mobile phone, or from your PC or Mac, or even from the internet.

Pictures

It's now easier than ever to spice up your presentation with images from your own photo library or from across the web. There's also an array of stock photos available from the ClipArt library to add a little more colour to your show.

Video

Videos shot on your own camera or even on your mobile phone can be seamlessly added to your show. If you've spotted an inspirational video you would like to include (using websites such as YouTube, for example) we will show you how.

Charts

With the help of a massive array of colourful and attractive styles, PowerPoint allows you to convert figures into easy-on-the-eye bar charts, pie charts, scatter graphs, line graphs, and so on.

Tables

Tables can fulfil the need to present data, such as sales figures, in a well-organized manner. It is much easier than you think to add that series of columns and rows to your slideshow and, with a host of design options, the result will look even better than you may have anticipated.

SmartArt

SmartArt is a relatively new addition to PowerPoint (PowerPoint 2007 and beyond) and allows you to convert text and data into flow charts or diagrams. These can help to get a message across in a more visual manner than text-based bullet points would allow.

OLDER VERSIONS? If you're using PowerPoint 2003, primitive versions of SmartArt can be added to presentations; they're called Diagrams.

Audio

It's easy to add a soundtrack to a presentation by selecting songs or

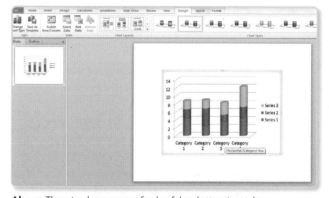

Above: There is a huge range of colourful and attractive styles to make your figures come to life in an appealing array of charts.

Above: Tables are a solid and versatile way to present information. It is simple to add columns and rows and the design options will make your data easy on the eye.

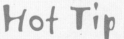

Hot Tip

Use a SmartArt chart instead of a bullet point list when presenting step-by-step information.

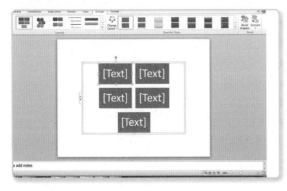

Above: Features such as SmartArt can help to bring information to life, making a welcome change from basic bullet point presenting techniques.

Hot Tip

Use animations when creating a quiz; there's no point in the answer appearing at the same time as the question.

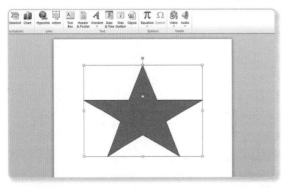

Above: You can add and customize your own shapes and boxes for each new slide.

sounds from your computer that will play at your command when you're delivering the information to the audience. A relevant audio clip can be a great way to keep viewers engaged.

Transitions

A stylish touch to keep everything flowing smoothly, transitions control how the slide show progresses from one slide to the next. You can have fades, flashes, wipes and dissolves, much like you'd see between cuts in a movie scene.

Animations

Like transitions, animations can also add a little icing to the cake by managing how objects appear within your slides; pictures can fly into the screen and then spin off with the click of your mouse. Animations are very important when controlling the order in which information appears.

Shapes and Drawing

Shapes, like text and picture boxes, often appear when adding new slides to a presentation. However, you can add your own shapes and boxes (rectangles, circles, etc.) when designing slides. You can also draw shapes like arrows and equation signs to help illustrate your point, and the line tool can also help you to draw freehand.

MOVING AROUND THE POWERPOINT WINDOW

Now that we're more acquainted with what PowerPoint is, what it is capable of and the ingredients available to us when creating a tasty slideshow, we're ready to take a look around the PowerPoint Window.

STARTING POWERPOINT ON A PC

Firstly, you'll need to open the software. Click Start (the Windows icon in the bottom-left corner), begin typing 'PowerPoint' in the search box just above and the PowerPoint icon (a document with an orange P clipped to it) will appear in a menu under 'Programs'. Move your mouse to hover over the icon and click.

⊖ Alternatively, you can click Start, followed by All Programs in the pop-up menu and then look for the Microsoft Office folder. Enter that folder and choose PowerPoint.

⊖ You can also use the mouse to double-click a 'shortcut' icon on your Desktop. In order to make this option available, use your mouse to right-click the PowerPoint icon and then select the Create Shortcut option.

> ## Hot Tip
> Once PowerPoint is open, right-click on the icon in the Windows taskbar (at the bottom of the screen) and select 'Pin this program to taskbar' to ensure it stays there for easy access even when the program is closed.

Above: It is simple to open PowerPoint from the start menu. From here you can choose to pin the programme to your taskbar or create a shortcut.

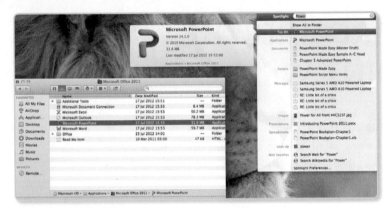

Above: On a Mac you can find PowerPoint in the finder folder, in the dock, or by searching with the Spotlight search bar.

STARTING POWERPOINT ON A MAC

Installing Microsoft Office 2011 for Mac automatically places a 'P' icon for PowerPoint in the Mac OS X dock at the bottom or side of the screen (depending on your preference). Click it to open the program.

→ Alternatively, hit the Finder icon (the two-toned blue face in your dock), click Applications on the pop-up window and scroll down to Microsoft Office. Open that folder by double-clicking and in there you'll find PowerPoint (double-click to open).

→ Another way is to press and hold one of the Command buttons on the keyboard (they're either side of the space bar) and then hit Space. This brings up the Spotlight search bar. Type 'PowerPoint' and click when it pops up in the window.

Hot Tip

To ensure that the PowerPoint program stays within the dock, right-click (Control+Click), hover over 'Options' and hit 'Keep in Dock'.

THE POWERPOINT WINDOW

Once you've opened the software, you'll be presented with the main workspace, which is called the PowerPoint Window. Mac users will, by default, be presented with the PowerPoint Presentation Gallery before they can access the PowerPoint Window (*see page 57 for more information*). Absolutely everything you need to do within PowerPoint can be controlled or achieved from within this screen. The screenshot below represents what you'll see when you first open PowerPoint.

Current Slide

In the centre of the screen you'll see the Current Slide view, which represents, as the name suggests, what appears on the slide you're currently working on. When you open PowerPoint, there'll be only a single Title slide (as you can see to the right).

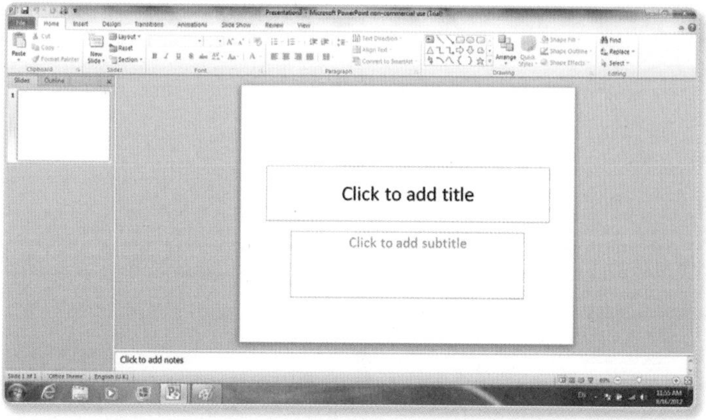

Above: This is what you will see when you first open PowerPoint.

Slide View

Within the left column of the window sits the Slide View. This is where each of your slides will appear in a thumbnail view as you are working on your project, and the Current Slide is automatically highlighted in this section. Using the Slide tab, you'll see mini representations of your slides, complete with pictures and charts. Clicking Outline will make it easier to control the text, as it shows a more detailed view of the titles, subtitles and words that appear on the slide.

The Ribbon

With PowerPoint 2007, Microsoft introduced the Ribbon user interface that replaced traditional menus and toolbars used to access features in previous versions. Think of the Ribbon as our Mission Control centre.

On the PC version, you'll see tabs representing File, Home, Insert, Design, Transitions, etc. Clicking on these tabs will dynamically change the options available to you within the interface. For example, the Home tab features options such as adding new slides, selecting slide layouts, selecting text fonts and adding shapes. If you then hit 'Insert' next door, the Ribbon

Above: The different tabs and the options within them allow you to seamlessly work through the different stages of your presentation.

Hot Tip

Play around with the Ribbon by selecting the various tabs and familiarize yourself with the options available within each.

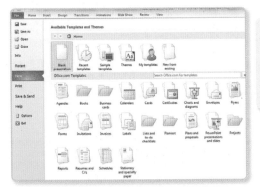

Above: File tab differs from the others and presents you with behind the scenes decisions, such as saving and printing, rather than layout and design options.

changes completely and allows you to choose charts, pictures, clip art, and so on. On the Mac version of PowerPoint, the Ribbon contains slightly different features (*see* page 34).

File Tab

The first tab within the Ribbon merits a little more explanation, as it differs so greatly from the others. Clicking File on a PC will bring up the 'Backstage View', which is named as such because it allows you to control the behind the scenes and, some might say, less glamorous aspects of the PowerPoint presentation. From here you can, among other things, save your presentation, send it to print and open older ones. There's more about the File tab, which arrived with PowerPoint 2010 and is a PC-only feature, within the Navigating, Opening, Saving, Closing section on page 35.

OLDER VERSIONS? As a precursor to the 'Backstage View', PowerPoint 2007 features the Office button, which contains much of the same functionality.

Quick Access Toolbar

The Quick Access Toolbar (QAT), as the name suggests, allows faster access to your favourite tools and commands, and it first appeared within PowerPoint 2007 with the new Ribbon interface. You can add more options, but the default tools are: Save,

Undo, Redo and Print. As you can see from the screenshot below, Mac users have a much fuller QAT from the start.

> **OLDER VERSIONS?** PowerPoint 2003 also has a default toolbar, which sits below the basic menus, featuring a host of common commands such as Save, Print, New Slide, etc.

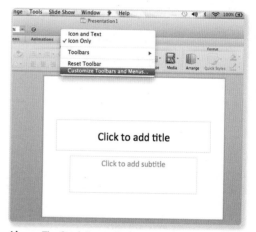

Customizing the QAT

In order to add items like Quick Print, Email and Open Recent File to the QAT on the PC, click the small arrow positioned to the right of the items currently residing in the toolbar to access the drop down menu seen in the screenshot on the right. Tick the item you want to add to the QAT. The More Commands option helps you add further commands.

Above: The Quick Access Toolbar allows you to customize the tools and commands that you use most frequently.

Notes Tab

At the bottom of the PowerPoint Window you'll see a thin text box beneath the current slide containing holding text reading 'Click to add notes'. Click within this box to enter the notes pane. Here you can type notes related to each of the slides. These won't appear in your presentation but can serve as helpful reminders when designing and presenting your slide show.

Status Bar

Beneath the Notes pane and within the PowerPoint Window's border, the Status Bar offers a few key details regarding your presentation. They are, from left to right, listed below.

↪ **Indicator:** Explains which slide you're working within.

↪ **Theme:** Indicates which theme is currently in use.

Spellchecker: A tick or a cross within this button indicates whether there are spelling errors that need attention (PC only).

Viewing options: Clicking each of these small boxes changes how your presentation appears on the screen. The default is Normal View but you can also select Slide Sorter, which makes it easy to rearrange the order of your slides, or Reading View (PowerPoint 2010 for PC only), which maximizes the size of the slide to fill the PowerPoint Window. The latter is great for practising your presentation. The final option is Slide Show view, which you should use when you're ready to showcase your work.

Zoom bar: Here you can toggle how large the current slide appears within the window. Hitting the 'Fit slide to current Window' tab next-door returns to the default view.

OLDER VERSIONS? In PowerPoint 2003 the Status Bar features a host of drawing tools, insert tools (pictures, text boxes, etc.), and formatting and style tools.

Above: In the 2003 version of PowerPoint the Status Bar offers a host of style and formatting tools.

Scroll Bars

These are displayed when there is more content within the window that can be viewed on the screen and are used to navigate around the presentation. They appear vertically to the right of your various panes (i.e. Current Slide, Slide View, Notes) but when you've zoomed in on a slide, a horizontal slide bar will also appear.

A CLOSER LOOK AT THE RIBBON

As we've mentioned already, the Ribbon is the key to controlling PowerPoint and is a much more user-friendly and efficient way of accessing the key features of the program. In order to move between the various tabs, you can hover over the title with your cursor and click to reveal the new design, formatting and viewing tools within. Here's a quick look at what you can do within each tab, but there's much more on this in Chapter two (*see page 47*).

- **Home:** Add new slides, copy cut and paste content; change the font, alignment, style and size of text and draw shapes.

- **Insert (PC only):** An easy way to add pictures, videos, audio, new text boxes, screenshots shapes, charts, tablets, ClipArt, WordArt, as well as headers and footers, dates, symbols, equations and more.

- **Design (called Themes on Apple Mac):** Adjust the project's theme, colour scheme, font group, theme effects and the style of slide backgrounds. You can also adjust the page set-up and slide orientation.

- **Transitions:** Control how the slide show progresses (Fade, Push, Wipe, etc.) and adjust the direction and speed at which a transition moves.

- **Animations:** Drop animations and effects that control how items appear within and leave the slides (i.e. Fly In, Fade In). You can also control the duration and order of these effects.

- **Slide Show:** Play your presentation, rehearse its timings and prepare it for broadcasting online.

- **Review:** Before you complete your show, you can check spelling, research facts, translate into new languages and add comments.

Above: The Ribbon tab allows you to control and access design and formatting features effortlessly.

Above: The Ribbon tab options for Mac differ slightly from those for a PC.

Hot Tip

If you're working with multiple presentations on a PC, you can neatly showcase them all on screen at the same time by selecting the 'Arrange All' button within the View tab.

View: Change how your presentation appears on screen, open Master views and adjust colours.

Additional Tabs

Invariably, new tabs will appear within the Ribbon as you work with PowerPoint; for example, when clicking within a content box on a slide, a new Format (Drawing Tools) tab appears. This presents options to draw and edit shapes, customize the style of those shapes and add WordArt. We'll explain these as we come to them.

The Ribbon on the Apple Mac

Mac users will see a slightly different set of Ribbon tabs. For starters, the File tab still resides within the familiar Apple menu bar rather than in the Ribbon, while the View tab is also AWOL. Some of the other differences are listed below.

Home: As well as adding new slides, adjusting text, and so forth, the Home tab is also the way of inserting pictures, video, charts and other media.

Format: The same as the PC tab mentioned above but here it has a permanent place within the Ribbon.

Tables, Charts, SmartArt: Instead of being placed in the Insert tab, these three features are granted their own tabs.

NAVIGATING, OPENING, SAVING AND CLOSING

Now that we're familiar with our surroundings within the PowerPoint Window and have untangled the Ribbon user interface, let's try our hand at navigating around the PowerPoint software and exploring some basic navigational and housekeeping functionality before we create our first presentation.

THE CURSOR

When you wave your mouse around within the PowerPoint Window, a small arrow moves around with you. Stopping and hovering over an icon, menu or feature allows you to click and select that item. The arrow appears most of the time when navigating around PowerPoint but, within the software, the cursor takes different forms depending on what you're doing.

- **Arrow**: Used for selecting items, menus and features.

- **'I' cursor**: Displayed when working within text or tables.

- **Up/down arrow**: Appears when extending a text box/shape vertically.

- **Left/right arrow**: Appears when extending a text box/shape horizontally.

- **Up/Down/Left/Right arrow**: Appears when moving a box/shape/item.

Scrolling

In order to move up and down (or left to right) within a scroll bar (*see* page 33), use your mouse to click the arrows at each end. For more precision you can grab the scroll bar with your mouse or trackpad (click and hold the left button) and move it up/down/left/right.

THE BACKSTAGE VIEW

If the Ribbon represents the functioning organs of the PowerPoint software, the Backstage View is the backbone (PC only). Within the Backstage View in PowerPoint 2010 you can find all of the key information about your current presentation, while a tab on the left-hand side gives you access to a host of essential options. Click the File tab on the Ribbon to see the Backstage View.

Info Screen

When you hit the File tab and enter Backstage View, the Info section is automatically highlighted. It's located halfway down the left-hand side menu and is highlighted in orange. From there you'll be able to perform some of the more advanced functions from the drop-down menus, which we'll tackle later but are listed here for reference.

- **Permissions**: Add a password to stop others accessing or editing the presentation and mark it as complete so collaborators know not to change it.

- **Prepare for sharing**: Inspect the document to ensure there's no unwanted personal information, make it disability friendly and check that it'll work with previous versions of PowerPoint.

- **Versions**: A new feature in PowerPoint 2010. Here you can recover previous versions of the file and, if AutoSave is enabled, you can recover documents that you closed without saving.

- **Properties**: In the pane to the right of the screen you can, among other things, add authors, and see file sizes, last saved date and last modified date.

Above: The Info section in Backstage View is automatically highlighted when you enter the File tab.

Other Backstage View Features

There's plenty more to do backstage, as illustrated by the tabs on the left-hand side of the screen. In order to access them, click the relevant tab and you'll see new options present themselves to the right of the screen.

Save: Ensure the latest version of your presentation is stored securely.

Save As: Save a newer version of your presentation, but under a different file name.

Open: Open an existing PowerPoint presentation.

Close: Close the Presentation (if you haven't saved it yet, you'll be prompted to) but not the PowerPoint program.

Recent: From this menu you can access your most recent pieces of work within PowerPoint. Double-click on the icon that looks like the letter P clipped to a document to open.

New: When you click this tab, you'll be presented with a newly populated menu offering you the chance to start a new presentation from a host of template options (*see* page 55).

Print: Access print options, such as how many copies to print, which printer, how many slides per page, colours and more.

Save & Send: There's a whole host of things you can do here, some of which we'll cover as we progress through the book. They include saving your presentation online to access it on any computer and broadcasting it to the internet.

Help: Access Microsoft's Get Started guide to help you with the basics and Office Help for more advanced assistance. You can also check for new software updates here.

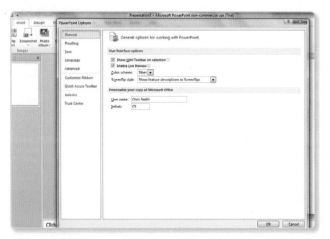

Above: New options will present themselves to the right of the screen when different tabs are selected.

Options: General and extensive PowerPoint options that will allow you to customize the Ribbon and the Quick Access Toolbar among other things.

Exit: Closes the PowerPoint program completely.

SAVING A PRESENTATION

Losing your work to a computer crash, breakage, theft or some other act of God is forgivable; however, losing weeks of meticulously crafted PowerPoint perfection through forgetting to save is not. There are several ways to ensure that, by regularly saving your work, you won't join the scores of unfortunate souls.

Hot Tip

In order to exit the File tab, click it again or hit one of the other tabs in the Ribbon.

Click the Save icon (the floppy disc) in the Quick Access Toolbar.

Use a 'keyboard shortcut' by holding down the Control key and pressing the S key. Keyboard shortcuts more often than not involve holding the Control key and pressing another – or simply pressing them both at the same time. In this case it's Control+S (or Command+S on the Apple Mac).

Hit the File tab and click Save.

If this is the first time you're saving your work you'll be presented with a pop-up dialogue box where you'll be asked to give your project a name and a location in which to save it. Type in the name you've chosen over the highlighted text that'll say 'Presentation 1' and click the OK box.

Above: When a file is saved for the first time, the Save As dialogue box will allow you to name your file and choose where to save it.

Saving a New Version of Your Presentation

If you want to save a new version of your slide show but keep the older one (this is useful if you're tailoring a similar presentation for different audiences), you can use the Save As functionality.

- Control+Shift+S (Command+Shift+S on the Apple Mac).
- Click File and select Save As.

Hot Tip

Give your project a logical name you'll remember and save it to a familiar destination such as your Documents folder. When you first save your presentation, that's where PowerPoint will want to put it. Let it do you a favour.

You'll again be greeted with a pop-up window where you'll need to give your new presentation a slightly different name, enter it into the dialogue box and then press Save.

POWERPOINT FILE EXTENSIONS

For the most part, this is something you will not need to worry about. However, when you save your presentation, you can add different file extensions to ensure your project will work on older versions of the software or on machines where PowerPoint is not installed.

Types of File Extension

A file extension is the lettering that appears after the dot when saving a file (for example, TestPresentation.pptx). When you first save your file, you'll see a drop-down menu that reads 'Save as type' (called Format on Macs) and here are some of the options to consider at this stage.

⊖ **PowerPoint Presentation (.pptx):** This is the default save setting. Files will work on computers with PowerPoint 2010 and PowerPoint 2007 but will not open on computers running earlier versions of PowerPoint, such as PowerPoint 2003.

⊖ **PowerPoint Presentation (.ppt):** Allows the presentation to open in any version of PowerPoint, old or new.

Above: There are various types of file extension you can choose, depending on your needs.

⊖ **PDF (.pdf):** This will allow the presentation to be displayed even if the computer you're using does not have PowerPoint.

⊖ **XPS (.xps):** Similar to the above but XPS was developed by Microsoft (PC only), whereas PDF was developed by Adobe.

Saving to the Cloud

Recent advances have made it possible to store our documents in cyberspace – or 'in the cloud', as it has become known. This has a number of advantages for PowerPoint 2010 users. It means you can access presentations when you're away from your own computer, share them with others and safeguard them in the event that your computer is lost, stolen or broken. Microsoft's cloud solution is called SkyDrive.

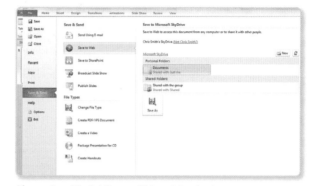

Above: On a PC, click Save to Web and then log in to your Windows account.

Accessing SkyDrive

In order to save a document to SkyDrive, you'll first need to be using PowerPoint 2010 for PC or PowerPoint 2011 for Mac and have a free online account with Microsoft. This can be a Hotmail email account, Outlook.com account, a Windows Live account, an Xbox Live account or a Windows Messenger/MSN Messenger account. The chances are, if you've spent

Above: You can save multiple documents on SkyDrive to be accessed when away from your own computer.

any time on the internet over the years, you have at least one of these (to sign up and get 25GB of free storage, visit Office.com).

⊖ **To save to SkyDrive on a PC**: hit File > Save & Send > Save to Web and then log in to your Windows account.

⊖ **To save to SkyDrive on a Mac**: hit File > Share > Save to SkyDrive and log in.

OPENING A PRESENTATION

When you open the software you'll be presented with the blank PowerPoint Window. In order to access presentations you've previously worked on, choose one of the following options and then click on the file name of your choice to recommence work on that slide show.

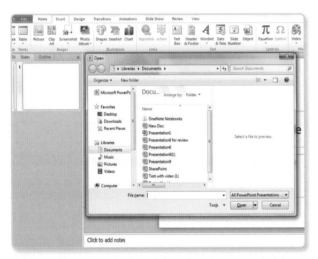

Above: From the Open dialogue box, documents which have already been started can be accessed and opened.

⊙ Use the keyboard shortcut Control+O (Command+O on the Mac).

⊙ Click the File tab and select Open.

⊙ Click the File tab and hit Recent (hit File then Open Recent on the Mac).

⊙ Open your Documents folder (or wherever you've stored your presentation) and double-click the relevant file. This will open PowerPoint with your chosen project.

Hot Tip

Mac users take note: whenever you see a keyboard shortcut that asks you to press Control + another key, for you this means pressing Command (the two keys either side of the space bar) + another key.

CHANGING THE SIZE OF THE POWERPOINT WINDOW

Viewing other items on your computer can be made a little easier by minimizing or reducing the size of your PowerPoint Window. This can be achieved by using the tools in the top right corner of the window (or the left for Mac users).

 Minimize: Clicking the 'minus' icon will keep your presentation open but send it to the taskbar at the bottom of the screen (into the dock on Mac). To restore it, click the PowerPoint icon within the taskbar.

Restore Down: Clicking the two-box icon (a green '+' on the Mac) will reduce the size of the PowerPoint Window to around half of your screen size.

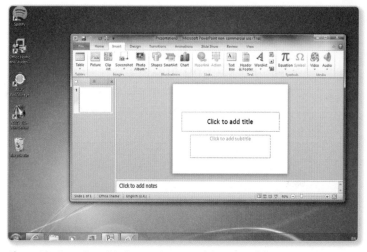

Above: The PowerPoint Window can be restored down from full screen to around half the screen size.

Maximize: Hitting the single square box icon (which appears when the window is restored down) will make PowerPoint appear in full screen view.

CLOSING POWERPOINT

After a lengthy session of hard work crafting your PowerPoint presentation, it can be satisfying to close everything down and put your feet up or, in many cases, start work on something else. Here's how.

1. Click the X in the top right corner to close the current presentation. If you only have one presentation open, this will close the PowerPoint program.

2. Similarly, use the keyboard shortcut Control+W (Command+W on Mac) to close the presentation you're working on.

3. Click the File tab and then Close on the left-hand side to close the current project.

4. Click the File tab and then Exit to close the program (File and then Quit PowerPoint on the Mac; the Command+Q short cut also works here).

5. Right-click the icon in the taskbar (dock on a Mac) and hit 'Close window' (Quit).

Accidental Closing and AutoSave

If you have unsaved changes to your presentation, PowerPoint will also issue a pop-up warning and give you the opportunity to save. However, sometimes software and computers can crash, but don't worry: you won't lose everything if AutoSave is enabled. PowerPoint automatically background saves your presentation every 10 minutes and will keep the last AutoSaved version if the program ever closes without saving. In order to access the AutoSave settings and alter how often your work is backed up, hit File > Options > Save (PowerPoint menu > Preferences > Save, on the Mac).

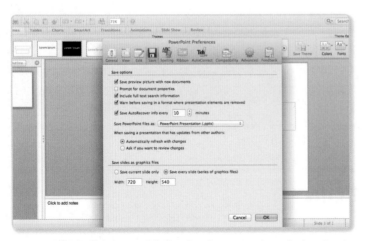

Above: The settings of the AutoSave function can be easily altered, such as how often documents are backed up.

OLDER VERSIONS? If you're using PowerPoint 2003, you can access the AutoSave settings by selecting Tools > Options. In PowerPoint 2007 hit Office Button and then PowerPoint options.

OBTAINING POWERPOINT

The fact that you're already reading this book has led us to the assumption that you've already got PowerPoint on your PC, but if you haven't, there are a number of ways to get it.

- **Download the software online:** To get the software right now, without leaving your keyboard, point your web browser (Internet Explorer, Google Chrome or Firefox) to Office.com/buy. You can download the software and install directly to your PC or Mac.

- **Get a hard copy:** For the best deal on a Microsoft Office package, your best bet is probably Amazon.co.uk (amazon.co.uk) but your local PC World or Currys Digital should also be well stocked. You can buy a software key to validate the downloaded version or a disc to install it the old-fashioned way.

- **Free trials:** If you want to try before you buy, or just use PowerPoint for a limited amount of time, Microsoft offers a 60-day trial of the entire Office 2010 package for PC (30 days on the Mac). Head to Office.com/try and follow the instructions.

Above: At Office.com/try a free trial of Microsoft Office 2010 is available.

CREATING A PRESENTATION

FROM START TO FINISH AND EVERYTHING IN BETWEEN

In this chapter we'll give you all of the information necessary to create and present a basic, text-based PowerPoint presentation. You'll learn how to edit and add slides, while employing themes and templates that will add style to your slide show. We'll also explain how to print handouts for your audience and illustrate the different ways to present your creation.

STARTING A NEW PRESENTATION

Once you've opened the PowerPoint software on your PC or Mac (*see page 27*), you will automatically be greeted with the PowerPoint Window and a brand-new presentation, just waiting to be customized. However, if you have opened an old presentation and want to start a brand-new blank one, hit the shortcut Control+N or Command+N for Mac users.

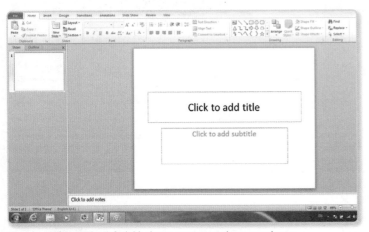

Above: The default blank presentation window is very basic.

The Blank Presentation PowerPoint Window

This default setting, with which we will be working initially, features the simple Office theme, which has no design bells or whistles. It contains a single Title Slide, which invites a title and a subtitle for your presentation with the message 'Click to add text'.

CONFIGURING PAGE SET-UP AND SLIDE ORIENTATION

After all of this build-up, you must certainly be eager to start filling those text boxes and begin adding slides. However, there are a couple of housekeeping matters to take care of, such as page set-up and orientation of slides. Configuring these early on is important, as they can affect the look and feel of your slides later on when you've already added content and here's how.

⊖ **PC**: Hit the Design tab in the Ribbon. On the left-hand side are the Page Set-up and Slide Orientation options. Click either to access the settings.

⊖ **Mac**: Select the Themes tab from the Ribbon and click the Page set-up/Slide Size button on the left of the screen.

OLDER VERSIONS? PowerPoint 2003 users can configure page set-up from File > Page Set-up.

Slide Orientation

You can change the layout of your slides from the default Landscape view to Portrait. Most commonly, PowerPoint presentations are Landscape, but if you plan to create letter-headed paper, for example, you'll need to go Portrait. In order to carry out this change, select the drop-down menu within Page Set-up.

Hot Tip
Within the Page Set-up pop-up, you can also select whether Notes and Handouts will be printed in Portrait or Landscape.

Slide Sizes

When adjusting the size of your slide, you need to take into account where you'll be presenting your slide show.

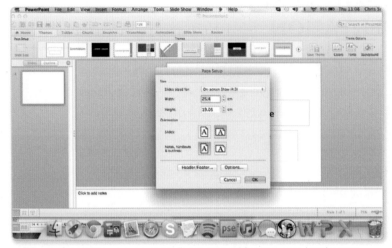

Above: Slides are automatically set up at a 4:3 aspect ratio, but the ratio can be changed (as seen here on a Mac).

Above: Slides are automatically set up at a 4:3 aspect ratio, but the ratio can be changed (as seen here on a PC).

The default setting shows slides at an aspect ratio of 4:3 (your TV from 15 years ago), but your computer/laptop screen is likely to be 16:9 (your TV now). If you're planning to present your work on a widescreen TV (see page 74) then you might want to opt for the 16:9 or 16:10 settings, which will ensure your presentation will fill the screen. Otherwise, there will be black borders either side of your work.

You can also manually adjust the width and height of slides, but there's no need for us to concern ourselves with this. In order to adjust the aspect ratio of slides, select Page Set-up and choose from the drop-down 'Slides sized for' menu.

OLDER VERSIONS? PowerPoint 2003 doesn't recognize widescreen aspect ratios.

THEMES AND TEMPLATES

Themes and templates are attractive design pre-sets that allow you to add a colourful flavour to your presentation. They're extremely easy to insert and there are loads to choose from to suit the tone and purpose of your slide show perfectly.

WHAT ARE THEMES?

Think of PowerPoint themes as if you were completely redecorating your home. Not every room is going to be the same, but even the most amateur interior decorator would want there to be some sort of style consistency throughout the house. Without a PowerPoint theme, you're simply placing the furniture (words, pictures, video, etc.) in white-painted rooms without coloured paint, wallpaper, borders or that stuff that makes an empty house your home.

OLDER VERSIONS? Themes don't exist within PowerPoint 2003; however, you can select slide design by selecting the Design button from within the formatting toolbar.

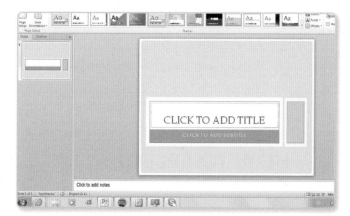

Above: PowerPoint themes, such as the Apothecary theme seen here, add style consistency to the slides.

WHAT'S IN A THEME?

There are a number of elements that combine to comprise a theme in PowerPoint. Most of them are there to make life easier for the user and to ensure that the presentation maintains a universally attractive and co-ordinated form. Chapter three is loaded with information on how to customize your theme with the following.

- **Colours**: Each theme has a colour scheme, which helpfully brings together a series of shades that work well together. However, you can select from a number of different colour schemes that also bring together co-ordinated colours.

- **Fonts**: Just like with colours, there are certain fonts that work well together. Themes combine them, with one font for headings and another complementary font for content text.

- **Slide layouts**: Within PowerPoint there are a number of pre-set slide layouts that you can select when adding new slides (*see* page 61). For example, there are Title slides, Title and Content slides (which allow you to type a title and then add a content item below), and so on. Each theme presents these layouts in a slightly different way.

- **Background styles**: As well as the above, each theme boasts its own background style that sits behind all of the content. This menu contains available colours and gradient shading for your slides, which will help to avoid nasty colour clashes.

HOW TO SELECT A THEME

From your Blank Presentation Window you can choose a theme before you start adding content to your slides. Select the Design tab (called the Themes tab for Mac users) from the Ribbon and a number of colourful suggestions will present themselves as thumbnail slides.

Hot Tip

Hovering over the various themes with the cursor automatically offers a view of how your presentation will look with that theme, helping you to decide which one is most suitable.

Click on a thumbnail and your presentation will adopt that theme. In order to examine all 40 themes built into PowerPoint 2010, use the scroll arrows or click the downward pointing arrow beside the thumbnails (on the Mac there's a drop-down menu that sits in the middle of the Theme bar in the Ribbon. To select it, click the down arrow).

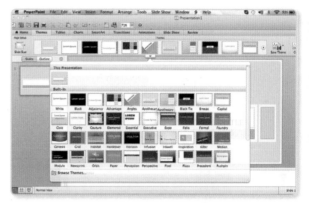

Above: A variety of themes, presented as thumbnails, are available to view.

WHAT ARE TEMPLATES?

Earlier in this chapter, we compared the use of themes in PowerPoint to decorating your house. Templates take a theme to the next level: using a PowerPoint template not only decorates the house but it also chooses and neatly arranges all the furniture for you. It is the easiest way to create an attractive presentation without worrying about designing slides. For example, see the Training New Employees template in slide sorter view in the screenshot (right).

Above: Templates are an easy way to create attractive presentations.

WHAT'S IN A TEMPLATE?

A template presents the user with an entire series of pre-designed slides, created with the same look and feel. All transitions and effects are also added to the presentation (*see* page 116).

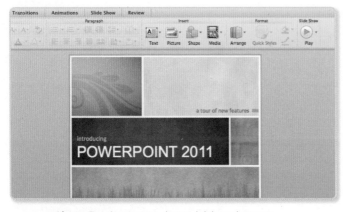

Above: Templates are pre-designed slides with generic content to be replaced by the user.

However, unlike Themes, there are a pre-determined number of slides, which are already filled with generic content. It's up to you to replace that content with your own words, pictures, SmartArt and charts, etc. As is the case with Themes, though, each template can be customized with a colour scheme and font scheme of the user's choosing.

START A NEW PRESENTATION FROM THEMES AND TEMPLATES

As you work with PowerPoint, you'll find it's best to make your theme/template choice before adding all of the content to your presentation. We would advise picking a theme and sticking to it, as chopping and changing can alter the appearance of your content (and not for the better). Beyond the Blank Presentation option, here is how you can select a theme or template when creating a new project.

- **PC Users**: Enter the Backstage View by clicking on the File tab then select New from the menu on the left and you'll see the available templates and themes.

- **Mac Users**: Select the File menu and click on New from Template (Command+Shift+P) to bring up the PowerPoint Presentation Gallery.

OLDER VERSIONS? PowerPoint 2003 has Design Templates available too. In order to pick one, click File > New and select New from design template. In PowerPoint 2007, hit the Office button then hit New and select from the templates menu.

Selecting a Theme or Template

For PC users, within the Backstage View there are a number of theme and template options within the New section. The following are available to PowerPoint 2010 users.

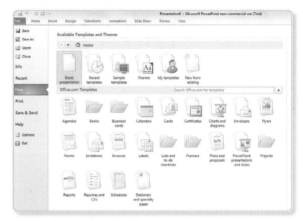

Above: There are a number of template or theme options available to choose.

➔ **Blank presentation:** The default no-frills blank canvas option. In order to select this option, just double-click it with your mouse.

➔ **Recent templates:** If you've already been working within a particular template style they will be listed within this menu; double-click to use again.

➔ **Sample templates:** Unlike themes, you cannot choose a template from within the presentation; it has to be done in Backstage View. Here you'll be presented with options for commonly used templates within Microsoft PowerPoint. Some of these include Photo Albums, Pitchbooks and Quiz Shows.

➔ **Themes:** Creating a template from a theme will display the first slide within a present design and all future slides you add will follow that design language.

➔ **My templates:** This section houses the templates you've worked on and saved, perhaps with some changes to those offered in the Sample templates menu (*see* page 129).

➔ **New from existing:** This option is useful if you've created a presentation that you need to tailor for a slightly different purpose. Selecting this will bring up a dialogue box asking you to select a previously saved file. Double-click the presentation of your choice in order to create a copy on which you can work without changing the existing file.

Hot Tip

In order to save a template you've been working on so you can use it in future, hit File > Save As and then select the drop-down 'Save as type' menu and select the PowerPoint Template (.potx) option.

Above: Templates can be saved to be reused in future.

Above: Office.com templates can be downloaded for less conventional uses such as invitations or menus.

OLDER VERSIONS? PowerPoint 2007 users will see a slightly different set of options when they hit the Office button followed by New; they include 'Blank and Recent', 'Installed Themes' and 'Installed Templates'.

Office.com Templates

Beneath the initial themes and templates options is the Office.com Templates section. These templates have been created by the community of PowerPoint users rather than by Microsoft and they have some more unconventional uses (invoices, CVs, birthday invitations, stationery envelopes, to-do lists.). They work in the same way as templates but need to be downloaded before use.

New Presentation on a Mac

Starting a new presentation by using a theme or template is slightly different for PowerPoint users on the Mac. The PowerPoint Presentation Gallery will automatically appear when you open the software; alternatively, hit the keyboard shortcut Command+Shift+P or select 'New From Template' from the drop-down File menu to access it at any time.

The Mac Theme/Template Selection Window

As you can see from the screenshot below, things are presented a little differently and, arguably, more effectively for Apple users.

→ By moving the mouse cursor over the various theme/template thumbnails you can see a moving visualization of the different slide designs it can offer.

→ Upon clicking a theme or template, a larger thumbnail appears in a pane to the right. You can use the left and right arrows to move between the numbered slides and see examples of how your selection will look in a full presentation.

Above: The PowerPoint Presentation Gallery appears upon opening PowerPoint on a Mac.

→ Select colour, font, page set-up and slide size by toggling with the settings in the drop-down menus in the pane to the right or the window. By playing with various schemes, you can see how a certain colour or font scheme will look within the theme or template. It's also possible to set the slides to Standard (4:3) or Widescreen (16:9, 16:10).

Mac PowerPoint Presentation Gallery

These are the options that are available to you when accessing the PowerPoint Presentation Gallery on the Mac.

→ **All themes:** There are 58 themes to choose from in PowerPoint 2011 for Mac, including the default Office Theme. When you've found one that you're satisfied with, you can double-click the thumbnail.

My Themes: This will be empty at the moment, but if you create a theme you intend to use again you can hit the Save Theme button in the Ribbon while on the main PowerPoint Window. Those saved themes will appear here.

All Templates: All of the templates immediately available. There are 15 default templates.

My Templates: Empty for the time being, but once you've created a presentation, you will be able to save it as a template (*see* page 56).

Presentations: Identifies 10 of the 15 templates deemed more suitable to be used for presentations, such as Project Status Report or Contemporary Photo Album.

Guided Methods: Lists the five other templates that are suited to creating guides, such as Five Rules for Creating Great Presentations.

Online Templates: Hit the Online Templates title and you'll see a host of categories appear. Included are: Agendas, Books, Business Cards, Calendars, Cards, Certificates, Charts and Diagrams, Envelopes, Flyers, Forms, Invitations, Invoices, Labels, Lists and To-Do Checklists, Planners, Plans and Proposals, PowerPoint Presentations and Slides, Projects, Reports, Résumés and CVs, Schedules, Stationery and Speciality Paper. If you're connected to the internet, double-clicking an item of your choice will load it into a new PowerPoint presentation.

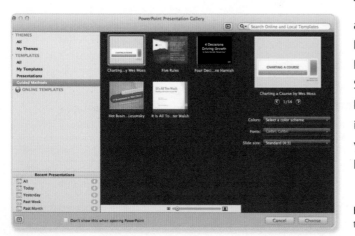

Left: Guided Methods lists the best templates to choose for creating guides (seen on a Mac).

ADDING TEXT TO YOUR FIRST SLIDE

We're ready to start populating our presentation with content, starting with text, and here's how to get going with your first PowerPoint slide. We've selected the Apothecary theme within PowerPoint (*see* page 51), so we shall proceed using that.

WRITING YOUR FIRST SLIDE

When starting a new presentation (Control+N), you're greeted with a single slide that appears in the Current Slide view and Slide View to the left. The slide has two text boxes, one for a title and one for a subtitle, currently filled with the words 'Click to add title' and 'Click to add subtitle'. Placing your cursor in these boxes brings up the 'I' cursor, which signifies an area where you can add text. A single click here will see the placeholder text disappear and you're ready to start typing your title.

Typing Within a Text Box

Once you've clicked within the text box you can use your computer or laptop's keyboard to start typing text. As with a word processor like Microsoft Word, words will appear on the screen as you type them. Once you reach the edges of the text box, further text will automatically move on to the next line.

Choose a Title

The first of the two text boxes you'll see on the screen is for your title, which should encapsulate the tone and content of your presentation. For example, if you're creating a photo slide show, the title might be 'Ellie's first Christmas' (or, in our case, 'My First PowerPoint Presentation').

Hot Tip

Try to keep the title within two lines of text to ensure that it doesn't break through the text box.

Above: Subtitles can be added to presentations to give extra information or identify the author.

Add a Subtitle

A subtitle for a presentation often simply identifies the author, especially if the presentation is an academic piece of work. In that case you would click into the text box and start typing your name. However, a subtitle could further clarify the content of the presentation. If your title reads: 'Getting to Grips with Microsoft PowerPoint', your subtitle might be 'From Novice to Grand Master in Two Weeks'.

Exiting and Moving Between Text Boxes

Once you've added your text, you can exit a text box by moving your mouse and clicking elsewhere on the slide. If this happens to be another text box, the cursor will enter this box and you can then start editing text within it.

Adding Text to a New Content Placeholder

When adding a new slide (*see* opposite page), you'll see boxes within slides just waiting to be filled. These are called content placeholders and can be used to add text as well as images,

pictures, videos, charts, audio and more, but the default setting is text. You can click within any content placeholder and start typing.

Here PowerPoint assumes that you want to use bullet points and will arrange your text as such every time you press the Enter key. The more text you add to the box, the smaller the text will get to ensure it fits within the content box.

Above: The default setting for content placeholders is text, so you can just click in any placeholder box and type away.

ADDING SLIDES TO YOUR PRESENTATION

In the previous section, we completed a text-based title page, but there's no such thing as a one-slide slide show, so in this section we'll help you add more slides and showcase the types of slides available to you.

ADDING A NEW SLIDE

The easiest way to add a default slide beneath your title page is to use the keyboard PC shortcut Control+M. You can also click the New Slide button on the left-hand side of the Home tab. A third method is to move your cursor to the Slide View and right-click (Command+Click on Mac); this will bring up a menu from which you can select the New Slide option. This new slide will appear directly underneath the title page in the Slide View to the left of the screen and replace your title page in the Current Slide View.

The Default Content Slide

Adding a new slide will automatically add the default content slide to your presentation. This slide features a pre-set title box placed above a versatile, multi-use content placeholder, which takes up most of the page. You can click within to start typing text but you can also insert tables, charts, SmartArt, pictures, Clip Art and video by clicking the different options. If you feel you're ready to start adding these items, head to page 137.

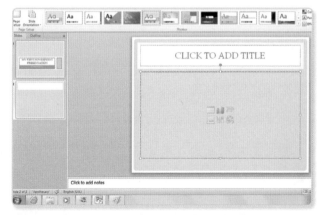

Above: A default new slide will feature a title box and multi-use content placeholder.

OLDER VERSIONS? In PowerPoint 2003, 'Insert content' options do not live with the placeholder; they're in the Status Bar toolbar.

SLIDE LAYOUTS

The default content slide that you see in the screenshot on the previous page is far from the only slide layout you can use. However, for our purposes of creating a basic text-based presentation it is certainly the best option.

Selecting a Layout When Adding a New Slide

Using the keyboard short cuts (Control/Command+M) will add the default content slide. In order to add a slide with a different layout, you can select the tiny down arrow beneath the New Slide button within the Home tab. This will summon a drop-down menu featuring the slide layout options. From there you can hover over and click to add your selection, which will appear directly underneath the slide featured in the Current Slide view.

Adding a New Layout to an Existing Slide

It's easy to customize a new or existing slide with a different layout. First of all, you'll need to identify the slide of your choosing within the Slide View tab; then right-click it and select the Layout menu to see your options.

Above: Slides can be customized with new layouts either by right-clicking on the slide or using the Home tab.

You can also achieve this by clicking the slide thumbnail to highlight it and then selecting the drop-down slide Layout menu within the Home tab.

Different Slide Layouts

We've already explained the Title Slide (see page 59) so here are the other eight pre-designed layouts you can add to a new or existing slide by hitting the Layout menu mentioned above.

→ **Title and Content**: This slide will appear as the default new slide. It features a title box and one for adding content of your choosing.

→ **Section Header**: These slides traditionally feature the presentation name and new section title.

→ **Two Content**: A header located above two content boxes side by side.

→ **Comparison**: Similar to the above, but with further title heads; great for comparing charts or photos.

→ **Title Only**: Aside from the title, a blank canvas.

→ **Blank**: An actual blank canvas.

→ **Content with Caption**: A title, text box and content box.

→ **Picture with Caption**: A simple way to illustrate a photo with title and corresponding text offering.

→ **Title and vertical text** (Mac only): Similar in appearance to the Title and Content layout, but text within the placeholder will run vertically down the page rather than across it.

→ **Vertical title and text** (Mac only): By default, all text content on the slide will run vertically.

Click icon to add picture

CLICK TO ADD TITLE

CLICK TO ADD TEXT

Within this slide I'd like to add a series of Screenshots about paramount and make jokes about staying awake during the presenta

Above: One possible slide layout is a picture box with a caption.

OLDER VERSIONS? PowerPoint 2003 actually has loads more pre-set layouts (29) than the two newer versions.

Duplicating Slides

In order to save you designing the same slide over and over again, Microsoft has helpfully added this tool that will copy everything over into a new slide. All you need to do is highlight the slide in Slide View, right-click and hit Duplicate Slide –or hit Control+D (Command+D on Mac) on your keyboard. The duplicate will appear directly beneath the original.

Rearranging Your Slides

The easiest way to rearrange slides is by using the Slide Sorter view (the tiny box in the Status Bar at the bottom of the page featuring four slides), which, once selected, will replace the Normal View. Here you can grab a thumbnail by clicking on it, holding down the mouse button and dragging it into a new position within the presentation.

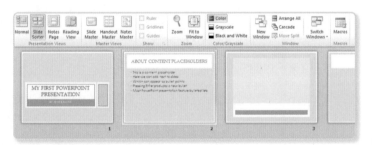

Above: The order of slides can be rearranged in the Slide Sorter view.

Deleting Slides

To get rid of a slide, just click on it within the Slide View and hit the Delete key; alternatively, right-click it and select Delete Slide. It's easy to do this by accident sometimes when you think you're editing content, so just hit Control+Z (Command+Z on Mac) to bring it safely back.

Moving Between Slides

Although you can only work on one slide at a time, you'll need to move between slides to read through your presentation and make amends. You can do this by using up/down arrow keys or by using the Slide View scroll bar. Once you reach the slide you'd like to view, simply click it.

NOTES

It's almost time to take the stage and deliver your presentation to your audience. In this section we'll cover how to add notes that will assist you with the all-important delivery.

ADDING NOTES TO YOUR PRESENTATION

As we mentioned in Chapter one, the Notes section sits neatly underneath your current slide in Normal View, with a 'Click to add notes' piece of holding text.

A good set of notes can help you deliver an effective and entertaining presentation, even if the note just reads: 'Relax, remember to smile and take regular sips of water.' Notes will not appear in your presentation, and you're the only one who'll see them. The idea is to print them off (*see page 70*) as a slide-by-slide guide for when you are delivering to your audience.

How To Do It

Hover your cursor within the Notes pane, click to bring up the flashing 'I' and then begin typing. Notes are unique to each slide, rather than for the project as a whole, so try to add comments that are relevant to the content highlighted on that slide. You can treat this box as a standard word processor.

What to Put in Your Notes

Since the bullet-pointed text within your presentation features only the major points you'll need to cover, there can often be a lot of information to commit to memory. Notes can

Above: Notes are unique to every slide so you can relate them to the different content in each one.

help with this. So, for example, if your bullet point reads: 'England won the World Cup in 1966', your notes could embellish with 'Bobby Moore was the captain, Geoff Hurst scored three times and they've barely come close since'. Other uses include the following.

⊖ **Jokes:** Reminders to add the humorous jokes and anecdotes you had planned.

⊖ **Script:** You can write an entire script out to read from. Although this will limit your ability to connect with your audience, it will ensure you cover everything.

⊖ **Design reminders:** Notes can help you plan how to build your presentation. For example, you could add: 'Remember to insert A-ha's "Take On Me" as a soundtrack'.

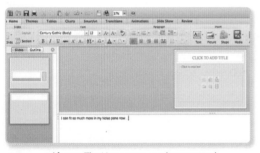

Above: The Notes pane can be increased in size to add more text.

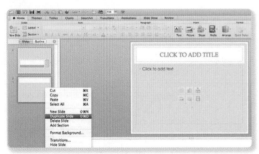

Above: To add extra Notes panes, duplicate a slide, then select Hide Slide from the Slideshow tab.

Increasing the Size of the Notes Pane

The Notes pane takes up a tiny portion of the available screen space within the PowerPoint Window, which – if you're adding a lot of text – could mean a lot of scrolling. You can increase the size of the Notes pane by clicking the border just above and dragging it up. In turn this will make the current slide smaller, but you'll have more room to view your notes.

Using Notes Page View

A more efficient alternative to altering the size of the Notes pane is to enter the Notes Page view, which features a smaller view of the slide and more space to type your notes. Select the View tab and select the Notes Page view from the left-hand side (Mac users can hit Command+3). You can return to the Normal View by hitting – you guessed it – Normal View within the Status Bar or Ribbon.

PRINTING A PRESENTATION

Although you'll be delivering your PowerPoint presentation from a laptop screen or an external screen, print-outs of your slide show can provide a valuable reference point for your audience, who can also then take them away. A paper reference can also be useful when practising the delivery of your newly created masterpiece.

QUICK PRINT A PRESENTATION

As is the case with most features within PowerPoint, there are umpteen ways to print handouts and an almost insurmountable number of settings that can be tailored to suit to your exact needs. Luckily, there's also a way to do it with just a couple of clicks – thanks to Quick Print. As the name would suggest, this is the fastest way to commit your presentation to paper.

How to Quick Print

Quick Print uses the default PowerPoint print settings or, if you've changed them within the Backstage View (*see* below), the most recent ones. Those default settings are: one copy, all slides, one slide per page, printed in order (collated) and in colour. It won't print any of your notes or handouts.

To Quick Print on PC, you'll first have to add the Quick Print tool to the Quick Access Toolbar (*see* page 31) and then hit the printer icon. Naturally, your laptop or computer will need to be already configured to hook up to a printer.

Printing Using the File Tab (Backstage View)

The command centre for all of your printing needs is the Backstage View within the File tab (or simply the File Menu on Mac/PowerPoint 2003). Hit File in the Ribbon and then the Print menu halfway down the left-hand pane. Below is the screen you'll see when preparing to print.

Above: The Print command can be found on the File Menu or Tab.

The Print Preview View

A large part of the Print screen within the File tab is the Print Preview, which is located on the right. Not only does this show how the presentation will look on paper, but it also dynamically updates to reflect changes to the settings. For example, if you switch from colour to grayscale (*see* page 72) this change will be instantly reflected within the Print Preview window. You can use the scroll bar or the page turning settings beneath the preview to move between slides.

OLDER VERSIONS? If you're on PowerPoint 2003 or 2007, there's no Backstage View so you'll have to use good old Print Preview: File/Office Button > Print Preview.

How to Print Multiple Copies

Click the up and down arrows; alternatively, click on the number 1 within the box, press delete and then type in how many copies you'd like to print.

Selecting a Printer

Here you can choose the printer you'd like to send the 'print job' to. Use the drop-down menu to select your printer.

Hot Tip

Hitting the Control+P (Command+P) keyboard short cut will take you directly to the Print settings.

Save to OneNote and Access Online

If you don't have a printer configured then the default option you'll see under the Printers heading is going to read 'Send to OneNote 2010'. OneNote is Microsoft's notebook software and comes as part of recent versions of Microsoft Office.

If you select this option and hit Print, an on-screen representation of the PowerPoint slides will open in the one OneNote software, and if you have your online SkyDrive account configured (see page 41), the presentation will automatically be saved to your online Documents folder at Office.com.

Printing All or Some Slides

Under the Settings drop-down menu section, within the Print tab, the default setting is 'Print All Slides'.

If you want to print just a section of your work, select Custom Range from the drop-down menu and then enter the pages you'd like to print (for example, entering 2–5 will print pages 2, 3, 4 and 5).

You can also print the Current Slide or select Print Selection. Here you'll need to enter the pages you'd like to print (for example, 1, 3 and 7).

Print Layout

From the Print Settings section within the Backstage View, which currently reads 'Full Page Slides' (one slide per page), you can select how the slides appear on

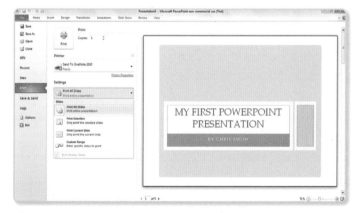

Above: You can choose whether to print the whole presentation or only a selection of slides.

a printed page, but within that top line you can also choose whether to print in Notes View (*see* below) or Outline View (*see* page 71, opposite).

OLDER VERSIONS? In PowerPoint 2003 and 2007, hit Print and select Notes Page or Outline View from the Print What drop-down.

Hot Tip

The best and most common setting when printing handouts is '6 Slides Horizontal', which will put six slides on each sheet of paper with the order running from left to right.

Printing Handouts

This setting is also controlled from the drop-down menu headed 'Full Page Slides'. Here you'll see a Handouts menu that allows you to select how many slides appear on the page. You can also tick a box that will add black frames to each slide, one which will scale up the slides to fill more of the page and another that will print high quality versions of the slides.

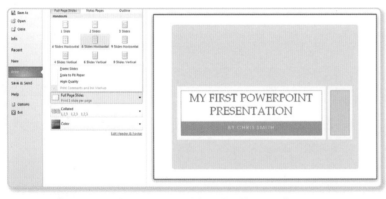

Above: For handouts, printing six slides ordered horizontally on a page is a good option.

Printing Your Notes Page

The whole point of having a Notes section is to print them out so you can use them while making the presentation. In order to do this, you need to select the File tab from the Ribbon and click the Print option on the left-hand menu. From there take a look at the Settings section. Hit the second drop-down menu that currently reads 'Full Page Slides' and change that to Notes Pages. Hit the Print button and a beautiful set of notes featuring a thumbnail of each slide shall be yours.

Printing in Outline View

Working in Outline view is something we'll cover in Chapter three, but we should mention here that printing in Outline View gives you a better view of the content within your slides, rather than the slides themselves. This can be a useful way to print in order to practise your presentation: simply select the Settings menu that currently says 'Print All Slides' and click Outline on the top row of options.

Collating Your Print Job

The Collated setting is useful if you're printing multiple copies of your presentation. The default setting is to print the pages in order (for example, 1,2,3, 1,2,3, and so on). Changing this setting to 1,1,1, 2,2,2, 3,3,3 will mean that all of the page ones will be printed followed by all of the page twos, etc.

Above: Notes pages can be printed out to help the speaker when giving the presentation.

Above: Slides can be printed in Outline View which focuses on the slide content.

Print Orientation

Select whether you'd like your slides to be printed in Portrait Orientation (vertically) or in Landscape Orientation (horizontally) on the paper. If you're printing single slides, the default

Above: Choose to print in either portrait or landscape orientation depending on your use.

Hot Tip

If you're opting to submit a print-out of your PowerPoint presentation as an academic piece of work then go for the full colour option – first impressions count!

Above: The print menu on a Mac offers the same print options as on a PC.

landscape view maximizes paper space, but if you're printing handouts, we'd suggest portrait as the best option.

OLDER VERSIONS?

In PowerPoint 2003 and 2007, hit Properties within the Print menu to choose orientation.

A Slice of Colour

Have you seen how much colour printer cartridges cost these days? In most cases, selecting the 'Grayscale' (uses grey shades rather than whites) or 'Pure Black and White' options will suffice for your handouts.

Printing Your Presentation on a Mac

There's no Backstage View for Mac users. Instead, you can click the printer icon in the toolbar to Quick Print or click File > Print (Command+P) to select the print settings. All of the PC options are present within a more minimalist menu, but the Quick Preview section, as it is called on the Mac, is much smaller.

PREPARING YOUR PRESENTATION FOR DELIVERY

You've created your first PowerPoint presentation, printed the handouts, got your notes and now it's time to present it. In this section we'll look at the best way to screen your presentation depending on your audience; we will also offer some guidance on rehearsing it and give some vital tips to ensure that the end product of your hard work is truly appreciated and enjoyed by all.

SHOWCASING YOUR PRESENTATION

Depending on your audience, you'll need to make a decision on how best to showcase your slide show. If you're delivering to one or two people then there's no doubt that your laptop or desktop monitor is a sufficient presentation tool. However, if you have an audience of work colleagues then you may want to hook up to an external monitor (like a flatscreen TV), and if you're speaking to a packed lecture theatre or conference hall then you'll definitely need the assistance of a projector linked to your computer.

Using a Computer or Laptop Screen

This is the easy part. You simply have to select the Slide Show view from the Status Bar in order to fill your screen with the PowerPoint presentation. This will minimize all toolbars, options, other views and menus, and simply display the slides.

Above: In Slideshow View the presentation will fill the screen.

MY FIRST POWERPOINT PRESENTATION

BY CHRIS SMITH

HDMI

Most recent laptops and all high definition televisions (HDTVs) or projectors have HDMI (High Definition Multimedia Interface) connection, which is the easiest – and most modern – way to link your laptop or computer to a television set. An HDMI cable can transmit pictures and sound from one to the other at higher quality than a VGA (Video Graphics Array) cable (see below). HDMI cables are inexpensive and durable. To ensure your computer or laptop has a HDMI output check the body for the port marked HDMI (it is shaped like the photo below).

Above: The HDMI port on a laptop.

VGA & DVI

No HDMI outlet? Your computer will still be able to link up with your TV or projector thanks to the VGA ports located on both machines. These 15-pin cables will transmit pictures but not sound, so you may need to add speakers to your computer to project sound. Rather than VGA ports, Macs use Digital Visual Interface (DVI) outputs, meaning you may need an adaptor as well as a cable to link your TV or projector.

Configuring Your Computer to Work on a HDTV

Connect your laptop or computer to your TV via HDMI or VGA and then use the Input button on your TV remote control to select the relevant channel. When using HDMI, the correct input will be HDMI (followed by the number of the input, e.g. HDMI2), whereas the VGA channel will likely be called 'PC' or 'Computer'.

From there, your PC should automatically recognize the presence of the TV but to tailor the settings hit Start > Control Panel > Hardware and Sound > Displays > Connect to an external display in order to bring up the dialogue box below. Depending on the PC you're using, these settings may be slightly different. Apple Mac users can adjust the display settings by selecting System Preferences > Displays.

Configuring Your Computer to Work with a Projector

Once you've connected the source and destination machine with an HDMI or VGA cable, you'll need to use the projector's remote to select the correct video

Above: Different display options can be chosen.

input (like the TV, it'll be called HDMI or PC). From here you should see an indication on the projected screen that the two devices are connected. Here's how to configure further.

- **Enter the Control Panel** (Start > Control Panel): select 'Connect to a Projector' under the Hardware and Sound menu. From here, you'll be presented with four further options.

- **Computer only:** Shows nothing on the projector screen and everything on your computer display.

- **Duplicate:** As the name suggests, this will mirror the same content on both screens.

- **Extend:** This view allows you to view different content on both screens. For example, in Presenter View (*see* page 76), you'll see the slides on the external display and a control screen on your laptop.

Projector only: The projector replaces your computer's screen (which will go black).

Above: These options dictate what content will be shown on the computer and projector screens.

Hot Tip

When connected to a projector, hit the Windows key + P to enter Presentation Mode (PC only).

Selecting Presenter View

When PowerPoint (from version 2007 onwards) detects that an external monitor has been connected, be it a HDTV or a projector, you'll be able to push the slide show itself on to the new display while commanding the presentation from your laptop screen. This is called Presenter View (select the Slide Show tab and tick 'Use Presenter View'); for a detailed explanation on how to use this see page 83.

Above: Presenter View displays the slide show on a monitor and allows it to be commanded from the computer.

Mirroring Your Presentation on Two Screens

Hit the Slide Show tab within the Ribbon on a Mac and you'll see a section dedicated to Monitors with the options 'Presenter View' and 'Mirror Show'. Selecting the latter shows the same content on the Mac and the external monitor.

However, it's less simple for PC users. Hit Start > Control Panel > Hardware and Sound > Connect to External Display and then from the Multiple displays drop-down menu select Duplicate these displays. *Et voilà*: you'll see the same information on both screens.

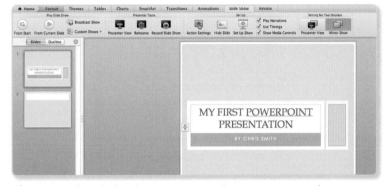

Above: Mirror Show displays the same content on the computer screen and connected monitor.

PREPARING TO PRESENT YOUR PRESENTATION

All the tools needed to make the final preparations before delivering your slide show reside in the Slide Show tab within the Ribbon. From here you can play your slide show from various points within the presentation, create a custom slide show, go hands-free and more.

Start Slide Show from Beginning

This tool, within the Slide Show tab, can be used when performing or practising your presentation. Hitting this button will play the presentation in full. You can move between the slides manually (*see* page 81) or automatically by adding timings (*see* Rehearse Timings on page 80).

Above: The Slide Show tab allows for final preparations to be made to the presentation.

Hot Tip

Use the keyboard shortcut F5 (fn+f5 on Mac) to begin your presentation from the first slide, from anywhere within PowerPoint.

Start Slide Show from Current Slide

Selecting this tool is a great option if you've built a long presentation and don't want to show it all or just want to practice a certain section without viewing the whole thing. Simply click once on the slide of your choice and then select 'Start Slide Show from Current Slide' within the Slide Show tab in the Ribbon.

Broadcast Slide Show

This isn't something we'll analyse in-depth at present, but PowerPoint 2010 allows you to give a presentation for online viewers to tune into (*see* page 208).

Custom Slide Show

Rather than spending all that time rearranging and duplicating (*see* page 64 for more information on both), you can create a custom slide show by placing slides in a specific order for presentation and repeating them if necessary. Click Custom Slide Show > Custom Shows > New and transfer the slides across one by one, by highlighting them and clicking Add. When you have finished, click OK and then Show to view the presentation in that order.

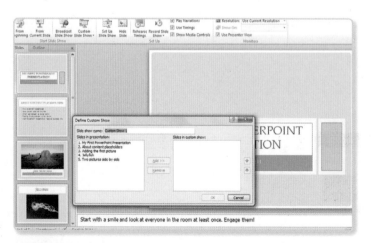

Left: Slides can be chosen, reordered and repeated to create custom shows.

SETTING UP YOUR SLIDE SHOW

The options in the centre of the Slide Show tab feature some more advanced presentation settings. In Chapter five, we'll discuss how to turn your presentation into a recorded video with audio narrations and highlighting through an on-screen laser pointer. Firstly, though, let's take a look at some of the more basic functionality available here.

The 'Set Up Slide Show' Window

This pop-up dialogue box, which is accessed by hitting 'Set Up Slide Show' in the Slide Show tab, features some basic and some of the more advanced functionality to be covered later. The following represent what is most relevant to us at present.

- **Show type:** Choose between Presented by a speaker (full screen), Browsed by an individual (window) and Browsed at a kiosk (window), depending on where your show will be displayed.

- **Show options**: For a presentation that will continue to run, for example at an information station, you can select the 'Loop continuously until 'Esc', meaning that it will continue to run until someone presses Escape on the keyboard to end the show.

- **Advance slides:** Select whether to move through slides by hand or via the pre-selected timings (we'll come to that shortly), which will enable you to go hands-free and 'work the room'.

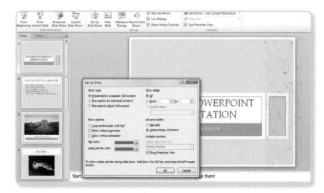

From this menu, you'll also be able to control whether narrations and animations play, the colour of your pen (when drawing) and the colour of the

Above: The Set Up Show menu allows control over how slides are changed and whether to run the presentation on a loop.

laser pointer (when pointing); additionally, you can select the Custom Show setting and adjust the external monitors settings (*see page 74*).

Hide Slide

Back within the Slide Show tab, this option simply hides one or more selected slides so that they won't be shown within the live presentation. They will not be deleted; they just won't appear in the show. It's great if you plan to use a presentation multiple times but feel that certain slides are not relevant to your audience. In order to undo this, simply right-click the hidden slide's thumbnail and deselect the Hide Slide box.

Rehearse Timings

Using this tool is a great way to give your presentation automatically without having to manually advance the slides. Hitting Rehearse Timings in the Slide Show tab will automatically launch the slide show and start a stopwatch in the top left corner of the presentation.

The idea is for you to deliver the presentation as you would on your big stage. When you're ready to move to the next slide or bullet point, hit Enter (or the down arrow on your keyboard) and PowerPoint will remember how long you spent on this slide. Continue this process throughout the presentation and when you're finished, press Escape.

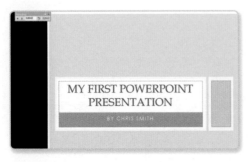

Now you'll have the full presentation recorded. You can review how long you spent on each clip by clicking the Slide Sorter view within the Status Bar. If you're unhappy, you can hit Rehearse Timings Again to have another go.

With the recording complete, selecting the Use Timings option from the Slide Show Ribbon tab will free you up to focus on the content rather than the technology when the time comes to address your audience.

Above: A stopwatch (top left of screen) will run on screen so that the presentation can be rehearsed and timings worked out.

DELIVERING YOUR PRESENTATION

You should now be ready for the most important part of this process: presenting to your audience. Here are the tools you'll need to pull it off successfully.

STARTING YOUR PRESENTATION

Regardless of the screen you're using to present your slide show (*see* pages 74–77), you'll need to press Start Slide Show from Beginning (or alternatively hit the F5 key, or fn+f5 on Mac) from the Slide Show tab to kick things off. Once you've taken the plunge, you're ready to start moving through the slides and engaging your audience.

Important Keyboard and Mouse Tools

Here are the key navigational tools, using both the mouse and the trackpad, when presenting your slide show to the audience.

- **To move to next slide:** Press enter; hit the space bar; use the down arrow; hit the 'N' key; hit page down; click your left mouse button; use the on-screen right arrow beneath the presentation (Mac and PC).

- **To move to previous slide:** Press Backspace; use the up arrow; hit the 'P' key; press page up; click the right mouse button and select 'Previous'; use the on-screen left arrow beneath the presentation (Mac and PC).

- **To return to start:** Press 1+Enter; right-click; select Go to Slide and enter 1 when prompted; hold down both mouse buttons (Mac and PC).

➔ **To jump to slide:** Press the slide number + Enter (for example, 9 + Enter).

➔ **To pause/resume manual slide show:** Press the S key (Mac and PC); right-click and hit pause/restart (PC).

➔ **To send screen to white or black:** If you'd like to pause and remove content from the screen for a while, you can make the screen black or white. Press 'B' for Black and 'W' for white, and hit the same key to bring the content back (Mac and PC).

➔ **To end the slide show:** Press the Escape key or press the minus key (Mac and PC).

MY FIRST POWERPOINT
PRESENTATION

BY CHRIS SMITH

Above: The keyboard and trackpad or mouse are needed to create a laser pointer.

Hot Tip
To change the colour of the laser pointer, click on Set Up Slide Show in the Slide Show Ribbon tab and select 'Laser pointer colour'. You can choose between red (the default), green or blue.

Using the Laser Pointer (PowerPoint 2010 for PC Only)

In order to activate the laser pointer, you'll need both your keyboard and your trackpad/mouse. Click and hold down both the control key and the left mouse button, and the on-screen dot will appear. Then move your trackpad /mouse to move the pointer around; let go of the button combination and the pointer will disappear.

How to Draw on Your Slides

In order to activate the pen tool, simply press Control+P (Command+P on Mac) while you're within your presentation, as this will change the arrow cursor into a pen. You can also right-click, select Pointer Options and then Pen (or, if you're on a PC, you can also select Highlighter so as not to draw *over* slides).

Once you see the pen icon replace the arrow cursor, simply hold down the left mouse button and scribble away by moving the mouse or trackpad. Pressing the E key will delete your doodles, while a single press of the Escape key returns the cursor to the arrow pointer (be careful, as two presses will exit presentation mode completely).

Hot Tip

You might consider it unthinkable to use a pen tool which would spoil your lovely slides, but it could come in handy to circle a particular stat or emphasize a particular point.

ABOUT CONTENT PLACEHOLDERS

- This is a content placeholder
- Here we can add text to slides
- Which can appear as bullet points
- Pressing Enter produces a new bullet
- Most PowerPoint presentations feature bulleted lists

Above: Certain information on slides can be emphasized with the pen tool.

USING PRESENTER VIEW

Presenter View is one of the neatest tools within the newer versions (from PowerPoint 2007 onwards). If you're presenting using an external monitor, it allows you to display your presentation slides full screen by using the television or projector you're hooked up to, while still accessing a full control panel on your host desktop or laptop computer.

When accessing Presenter View, ensure your computer is connected to the external monitor (*see* page 74–77). Once that screen is selected within the Monitor section of the Slide Show tab, you'll be able to tick the 'Use Presenter View' box. The presentation won't immediately load on to the external monitor but you'll see it appear on your television or projector when you hit Start Slide Show.

The Presenter View Window

With the first slide now present on your external monitor, your PC screen will then be furnished with the Presenter View which means you will see the following.

1. Current slide (left) so you can see what's on screen.
2. The Notes pane (right) so you can keep reminders of your talking points.
3. Slide show thumbnails (bottom) so you know what's coming next.

All the mouse and keyboard commands mentioned on pages 81–82 still work in Presenter View; you can also draw and use the laser pointer (PC only) on the 'Current Slide' pane, and your movements will be translated to the big screen as you make them. You will also be able to see the following.

Above: The computer screen will display various aspects of the presentation whilst the external monitor displays only the slides.

⊝ **Slide count:** for example, 'Slide: 4 of 7'.

⊝ **Time of presentation:** How long your presentation has been running.

⊝ **Time:** The actual time of day. Great if you're working in a classroom setting and need to finish by a certain time.

Left and right arrows: Use these to move between slides.

Pen icon: Hit this to select all of the arrow options (arrow pen, highlighter, ink colour).

Slide show: Effectively, this represents a right click and houses commands such as next slide, previous slide, pause, end show, etc.

Hot Tip

To ensure your computer or your external monitor does not time out and leave you with a blank screen when delivering a presentation, hit Start > Control Panel > Hardware and Sound > Power Options > Edit Plan Settings and then change the 'Dim the display' and 'Turn off the display' settings to 'Never'.

Zoom: Use the magnifying glass buttons to zoom in and out of notes.

Presenter View on Mac

Presenter View takes a slightly different form on Mac computers. The new screen, which is shaded black, and different to all other screens within PowerPoint (as you can see from the screenshot here), features only the next slide in your slide show, but all of the other features remain.

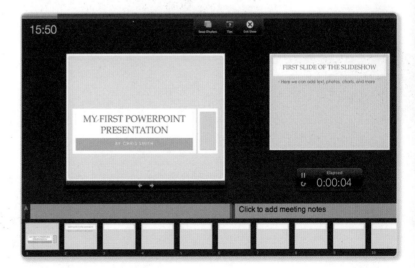

Above: Presenter View looks different on Mac computers.

IMPROVING A PRESENTATION

EDITING TEXT

After completing your presentation, it's likely that you'll want to make changes, additions and corrections to your text. In some cases, you'll want to delete it completely and start certain sections over again – here's how.

Above: Place your cursor where you want to start editing, click, and start typing.

Above: With the Ribbon select tool you can select everything or just certain objects.

ADDING TEXT

Just like when you were first adding text to a content placeholder, you can click within the box to select and edit text. The 'I' cursor will appear within the text closest to where you clicked, so if you want to edit from the end of the section, point your cursor immediately after the last word and click.

The Ribbon Select Tool (PC)

Within the Home tab, look to the right and you'll see a Select button with a cursor arrow; through this drop-down menu you can choose to Select All with just one click. This tool will also allow you to select objects, such as placeholders or pictures, or to bring up the Selection Pane where you can reorder the appearance of content.

Selecting a Section of Text

In order to change or apply new fonts or

Hot Tip

In order to select a paragraph of text, hit your left mouse button three times in quick succession.

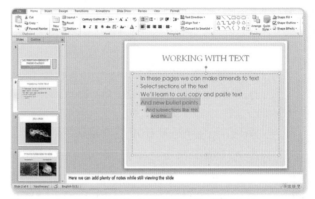

Above: Text can be selected by holding down the left mouse button and dragging the cursor over it.

formats to a word, sentence, paragraph or entire content placeholder, you need to select or highlight it. To select all of the text within a box, use the Select All shortcut Control+A (Command+A on Mac). You can also hold down the left mouse button, while the cursor is positioned where you'd like to begin selecting text, and move the mouse over that section.

Deleting Text

Select the relevant section of text and then press Backspace (Delete on Mac) to remove it. If you want to delete a single word or to correct a spelling, you can place your 'I' cursor directly behind that word or letter and press Backspace to delete one letter at a time.

Hot Tip

Backspace will remove text from right to left (anticlockwise), while the Delete (Fn+Delete on Mac) key will wipe out text from left to right (clockwise).

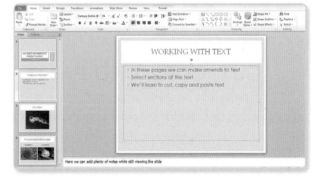

Above: Backspace removes text to the left of the cursor, while Delete removes text to the right.

Amending Text

In order to amend text, just click your cursor where you'd like to add the text and start writing; this will add to the content placeholder rather than overwrite what is already there. To type over old text, rather than adding to it, press the Insert button on your PC and then press it again once you're ready to revert back to the default Insert mode.

Adding a New Bullet Point

As we explained in Chapter two (*see page 60*), whenever you press Enter within a text box, a new bullet point will be added directly underneath. If you'd like to insert a new bullet point within a content placeholder, place your 'I' cursor at the end of the sentence above where you'd like the next point to appear and hit Enter; this will push those underneath down.

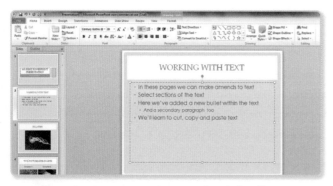

Above: It is easy to create sub-points within a bulleted list.

Adding Sub-points and Multiple Paragraph Levels

You can also use this tool to create sub-points (or second level points) within the list. Hit Enter at the end of a bullet point and then press Tab on the keyboard; this will indent the next point. You can do this multiple times.

CUT, COPY AND PASTE

The Cut, Copy and Paste tools are three of the most useful PowerPoint commands. They allow you to take text (or any other object) from one location, store it on a virtual clipboard and then paste it elsewhere within your presentation.

Copying Text to the Clipboard

Use the instructions on pages 88–89 to highlight the area of text you wish to copy.

Once you're happy with your selection, you can use the keyboard shortcut Control+C (Command+C on a Mac) to copy it to the virtual clipboard.

If you've copied multiple items, you)can access them all on the PowerPoint Clipboard (see right) which stores all of your recent copies. Clicking on an item within the Clipboard will paste it on to the slide in Current Slide View.

Above: The clipboard gives you easy access to recently copied items.

Cutting Text

The Cut tool has the same effect as Copy, in that it still copies the selected text to the Clipboard. However, in this case it also removes the text from the source. While Copy is best when used for duplicating text elsewhere, Cut is more efficient if you want to move a section of text from one slide to another. In order to access the Cut tool, select the section of text and hit the keyboard short cut Control+X (Command+X on Mac).

Hot Tip

When copying, cutting and pasting text, right-click the highlighted sections and hit the relevant command. Icon buttons for all three also appear in the Home Ribbon tab on PCs and within the Toolbar on Macs.

Pasting Text

Once you've copied or cut the relevant text to the Clipboard (see above), you can paste it elsewhere into the PowerPoint presentation. Simply position the cursor within the content placeholder and hit Control+V (Command+V on a Mac) and the text will appear, as if by magic, directly after where you placed the cursor.

Above: Clicking on the border of a content placeholder selects it so that you can delete it.

Deleting it All

If you want the whole content placeholder gone from your slide, use your mouse to click on the border and then hit Backspace or Delete (or use the Cut tool) and it'll be gone. However, if you do this by accident, read the section below, as this can rescue you. If you'd like to cut, copy and paste the text elsewhere, use the tools mentioned above.

UNDOING MISTAKES

There's nothing worse than the thought that, through some momentary insanity, you've deleted all of your beautifully crafted text. When messing around with Cut, Copy and Paste tools, these moments of panic can become common.

The Undo Tool

Thankfully, all is not lost as there is an easy fix to bring your work back. This tool works across the software, so keep it in mind if you delete a slide by accident, add a theme you don't like, change a font or decide a particular picture doesn't work.

- **On a PC:** Hit the back arrow in the Quick Access Toolbar to jump back one step (the keyboard shortcut is Control+Z).

Hot Tip

The small down arrow next to the Undo command will launch a menu that allows you to jump several steps back at a time – perfect if you're unhappy with a recent change of direction.

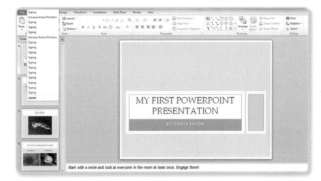

Above: The Undo command allows you to undo several actions in one go.

On a Mac: Hit the Edit menu at the very top of the screen and select Undo. The keyboard shortcut is Command+Z and there's also a button in the centre of the toolbar (the orange back arrow).

The Redo Tool

The Redo tool comes in handy if you've used Undo (see opposite) to take a step back but want to redo the undo. The keyboard shortcut is Control+Y (Command+Y for Mac) but you can also use the toolbar arrow next to Undo. Drop-down arrows in the toolbar allow you to jump forward several steps.

Don't Save It

If you're unhappy with your afternoon's work and want to start again from your last save, simply close the presentation (*see* page 43) and select 'Don't Save'. Then you can reopen the document to return to the last save (*see* page 42).

FINDING TEXT WITHIN YOUR PRESENTATION

If you know the piece of text you'd like to amend but don't want to spend ages poring through each slide to locate it, you can use PowerPoint's built-in finder tool. It lives within the Editing pane

Above: The finder tool makes locating particular words much quicker than scanning by eye.

Above: The find and replace tool on a Mac is very useful for correcting something several times.

of the Home tab in the PowerPoint Ribbon (PC only); select the binoculars to bring up the Find window.

From there you can type in the word of your choice and PowerPoint will highlight each of the destinations where that particular word or phrase appears. To move through the slides press Enter until you reach your preferred occurrence.

Finding Text on a Mac
Apple users have the advantage of an omnipresent Search in Presentation bar at the top right corner of the PowerPoint Window. Entering the cursor here (or using the Command+F shortcut) and typing will guide you directly to the section of your choice. Press Enter (or use the left/right arrows within the bar) until you get there.

Find and Replace
This tool very is useful if you know that there's something you'd like to correct multiple times throughout the presentation.

➔ **On a PC**: Press Control+F to bring up the Find window and hit the Replace button. Type a word (e.g. Powerpoint) into the 'Find what' box and type the correct replacement (e.g. PowerPoint) within the 'Replace with' box, and then click the 'Replace All' button.

→ **On a Mac**: Use the drop-down arrow on the Search in Presentation bar in the PowerPoint Window and follow the instructions above.

SPELLCHECKING YOUR WORK

If your presentation is littered with spelling errors, this will immediately undermine your authority. Thankfully, for those of us whose brain wasn't fitted with the complete *Oxford Dictionary* software, there are numerous tools to ensure everything is accurate.

Above: PowerPoint can check your spelling by underlining errors in red.

Spellchecking as You Type

If PowerPoint believes you've spelled something incorrectly it will underline it in red. Right-click the word; if PowerPoint has suggestions for the correct spelling you will see them listed in the pop-up menu. Hover over the correct spelling and click it. This action will replace the incorrect word with the correct one.

Spellchecker in the Status Bar (PC Only)

Within the Status Bar, at the very bottom of the PowerPoint Window, there is a small box that indicates whether spelling errors are

Right: A red cross in the status bar (top) lets you know there are errors, and green tick indicates there are no spelling errors (bottom).

present within your work (PowerPoint 2007 onwards). If there are no errors a tick will appear over the open book, whereas if there are errors that need your attention you'll see a red cross. Clicking the red cross will launch the PowerPoint Spelling tool.

Summoning the Spelling Tool

Beyond the red cross and red underline, you can check your spelling on PCs by selecting Review from the Ribbon and then hitting the nice big spelling button (which says 'ABC' and has a big tick through it). On a Mac, select the Tools menu and click Spelling or use the keyboard shortcut Command+Option+L.

Using the Spelling Tool

Let's imagine that in our presentation we've incorrectly spelled Microsoft as 'Mircosoft' and from the Window you can see that the software is suggesting we change it to Microsoft or perhaps the word Mycroft. Here's an explanation of the tools we can use here.

⊖   **Ignore**: Hit this button if you're happy with how the word is spelled. This will stop PowerPoint assuming that the word is spelled incorrectly.

⊖   **Ignore All**: If the word appears multiple times during the document, hitting this button will tell PowerPoint that you're happy with how it's spelled throughout the presentation.

⊖   **Change**: Hitting this button will change the word to the one listed in the 'Change to' box.

⊖   **Change all**: Will change the incorrectly spelled word to the highlighted suggestion throughout the document.

⊖   **Add**: Use this button to add a word PowerPoint thinks is incorrectly spelled to your dictionary, so that the software recognizes it next time.

Above: Words can be added to the PowerPoint dictionary to be recognized in future.

Hot Tip

You can also right-click on a word and select Add To Dictionary, which means PowerPoint (along with Word, Excel, OneNote and all Office programs) will add it to your custom dictionary and recognize it in future.

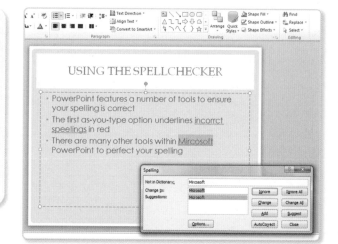

Above: PowerPoint offers suggestions for correcting the misspelt word.

Suggest: This prompts spelling suggestions.

AutoCorrect: Once you've highlighted the suggestion of your choice, hit AutoCorrect to make sure that PowerPoint will change the word automatically next time you type it incorrectly.

Close: Closes the Spelling window.

Completing the Spellcheck

Once you've addressed all of the errors that PowerPoint thinks you've made, the Spelling window will be replaced with a notification that the 'Spelling check is complete' – hit OK and continue with your work.

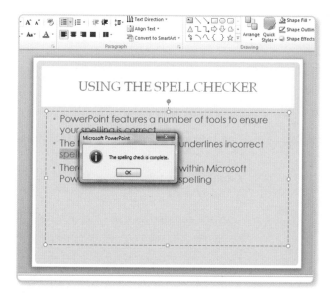

Above: The spellchecker will let you know when it is complete.

Above: You can choose your preferences for how spelling mistakes are automatically corrected.

AutoCorrecting Your Spelling

Occasionally, when you're typing within PowerPoint, you'll notice that the software automatically changes your text after you've finished writing a word. To access the full range of AutoCorrect options hit File > Options > Proofing > AutoCorrect Options (Tools > AutoCorrect on Mac).

⊜ **Show AutoCorrect Options buttons**: If PowerPoint AutoCorrects your text it will, by default, present a little lightning bolt beneath the word that gives you the option of overriding the changes or stop correcting that particular word.

⊜ **Correct TWo INitial CApitals**: This will make those unwanted second capital letters in a word go away.

⊜ **Capitalize first letter of sentences/table cells**: Some basic grammar help.

⊜ **Capitalize names of days**: No one wants to make grammar errors on a thursday.

⊜ **Correct accidental use of cAPS LOCK key**: This often happens when a user attempts to hit the shift key in order to capitalize the first letter of a word.

⊜ **Replace text as you type**: Ensuring this box is ticked enables PowerPoint's vast library of commonly misspelled words to lend a helping hand.

Exceptions: Adjacent to the first two options in this menu, you'll see a box that says Exceptions. Here you can add items where you don't want the first letter to be capitalized (e.g. anon.) and where using two capitals at the start of the word (e.g. IDs) is actually correct.

Replace/With: As you can see, this list shows a list of commonly used symbols such as ©, which is actually typed as (C), and ™, which is typed as (TM). You can use the tools in there to add your own items or delete from this list.

Using AutoFormat

While we're within the AutoCorrect options, it's a good time to take a look at the AutoFormat As You Type tab. This controls the AutoCorrect options outside of spelling and capitalization, such as when to hyphenate words or add internet hyperlinks. You can see the options in the screenshot to the right.

Apply as You Type Settings

From the window mentioned above you can also control whether PowerPoint automatically adds bullet points and numbered lists,

Hot Tip

PowerPoint's suggestions won't always be right, especially if you're using colloquial terms and proper nouns such as place names. If you're unhappy with a correction just press Control+Z (Command+Z) to undo it and move on with your business.

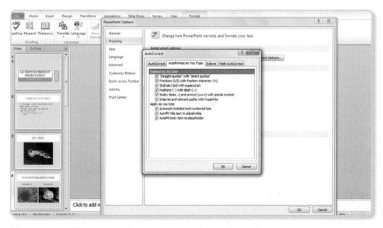

Above: You will be presented with options such as replacing hyphens with dashes.

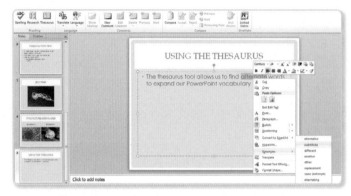

Above: If you need an alternative to a word used too often, the Thesaurus can offer suggestions.

whether to AutoFit title text to placeholder (PC only) and whether to AutoFit body text to placeholder.

Making Use of the Thesaurus

The Thesaurus tool is perfect for checking the meanings of words and finding alternatives (synonyms) to terms we use too often.

➔ Access the Thesaurus by right-clicking on the word of your choice and selecting Synonyms to reveal alternatives. Then select the word you prefer to replace it.

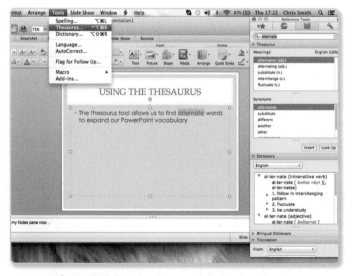

Above: The Reference task pane includes handy tools such as a dictionary and thesaurus.

➔ Right-click a word and select Look Up to launch the Reference Tools toolbar (Mac only). Here you will have the chance to look up a dictionary definition of the word, to consult a bilingual dictionary to obtain a translation from English and to access online research tools like Bing, Encarta, Answers.com and more.

➔ To launch the Reference Tools Task pane (*see left*)

Hot Tip

If your PowerPoint default language is English (U.S.) instead of English (U.K.) the software will think you've made a host of spelling errors. Altering the proofing language within the Language window will let PowerPoint know that you mean to 'customise' rather than 'customize' your language.

you can also hit the Thesaurus button within the Review tab (PC only).

Language

The Language button within the Review Ribbon tab can be important if you'd like to produce your presentation in a language other than English.

Translate

Within the Review tab in the Ribbon (Toolbox on a Mac), you can translate your text into another language. This tool can be handy if you're presenting to a diverse audience and would like to add content placeholders to encapsulate multiple languages. Simply select the text you'd like to translate, hit the Translate button in the Review Ribbon tab (View > Reference Tools > Translation on a Mac) and choose the desired languages.

Left: Make sure you are set up in the right language or PowerPoint will mistakenly think you have made spelling errors.

FORMATTING TEXT

Now that your text is spotless in terms of language, spelling and grammar, we can think about making it a little bolder, a little braver and a little prettier. Within the next few pages, you'll find plenty of information on improving the look and feel of your text.

TEXT EMPHASIS TOOLS

When editing text, you'll notice that the Home tab features most of the same formatting tools you'll see in a word processor like Microsoft Word. Some of the basic ones are listed below.

- **Bold**: Makes your text appear darker and slightly thicker. It's ideal to give single words emphasis or to identify titles. Select text and click the B icon in the Ribbon or hit Control+B (Command+B on Mac).

- *Italic:* Select text and hit the slanted I icon or the short cut Control+I (Command+I on Mac) to add emphasis to words or sentences.

- Underlined: Use the U Icon or hit the short cut Control+U (Command+U on Mac).

Above: You can emphasise text by making it bold, italic or underlined.

INCREASING AND DECREASING FONT SIZE

Sometimes it's necessary within PowerPoint to change the size of your text in order for it to fill out or make more room within your content placeholder. As always, with PowerPoint there are numerous ways to do this, but first of all you'll need to highlight the relevant text (see page 88).

Hot Tip

Hitting the drop-down menu gives you a number of underline options to choose from (dotted, double underline, etc.).

Above: The increase and decrease icons allow you to steadily change the size of your text.

The best way to steadily increase the size of your text is to use the dedicated buttons within the Ribbon. The font size icons (see in the screenshot above) will either increase or decrease the size of the text. You can also use the keyboard short cuts Control+Shift+> to increase or Control+Shift+< to decrease text sizes.

Alternatively, you can change the font size by using the drop-down menu that displays the current size.

Hot Tip

Don't make your text too small just to fit it on a slide. Instead, consider adding a new slide to make room.

TEXT ALIGNMENT

Text alignment concerns how your words will appear within the PowerPoint content placeholders in which they sit. There are four key options within the Paragraph section of the Home tab.

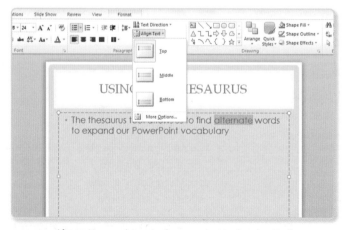

Above: There are a number of options for where words can sit in the content placeholders.

Above: You can determine how your text is placed vertically.

Align Text Left: The first word will hug the left edge of the box.

Centre Text: Places text equidistantly from the left and right edges of the content placeholder, with the middle letter anchoring the centre.

Align Text Right: The last word will hug the right edge of the box.

Justify Text: This option spaces the text out to ensure that the words are spread out evenly across the line.

Vertical Text Alignment

You can also select the Align Text box within the Home tab to choose whether your words are anchored to the top, bottom or centre of the content placeholder.

Text Direction

In the West we generally read and write from left to right, but in PowerPoint, anything goes. You may want a title to run from the top to the bottom of the page, or from the bottom to the top, for the purpose of building a heading (see below).

Before you go flipping your words on their heads, though, you'll need to ensure that your content placeholder has been designed (*see* page 128) in a way that would accommodate vertically aligned text; however, if that's up to scratch, you can select from four options within the drop-down box (*see* screenshot above).

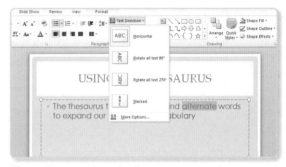

Above: You are not limited to having your text run from left to right.

- 🡒 **Horizontal:** The default text layout.

- 🡒 **Rotate all text 90˚:** Will change your text to run vertically from top to bottom (Rotate Clockwise on a Mac).

- 🡒 **Rotate all text 270˚:** Will change your text to run vertically from the bottom of the content placeholder to the top (Rotate Counterclockwise on a Mac).

- 🡒 **Stacked:** This hardly ever looks good (try it if you don't believe us). It will place all letters on top of each other.

Above: Text can be rotated to enable you to have sideways headings.

Hot Tip

Once you've made these changes and your text is running in the right direction, you may want to use the Align Text tab to ensure the words hug the correct portion of the content placeholder.

BULLET POINTS AND NUMBERED LISTS

You may have noticed when writing within content placeholders that each time you press Enter, a new bullet point is created, as PowerPoint assumes that most text slides will feature a number of bulleted talking points.

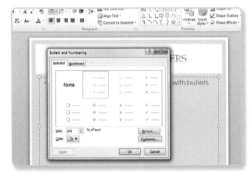

Above: Select the bullet options by highlighting your text and clicking on the adjacent icons in the Paragraph pane of the Home tab.

Above: You will find the numbered list options in the Paragraph pane in the Home tab.

In order to turn a text passage into bullet points or a numbered list, you can simply select the text and click the adjacent icons in the Paragraph pane of the Home tab. The type of bullet or number used will be linked to your theme, but you can select your own style from the drop-down arrow next to the icons (see some of the options above).

Getting Fancy with Bullet Points and Numbered Lists

In order to customize the appearance of bullets and numbers even further, you can select the Bullets and Numbering option (Define New Bulle' on Mac) from the drop-down menu found in both icons within the Paragraph pane.

Hot Tip

If you're continuing a numbered list from the preceding slide, change the 'Start at' number from within the Bullets and Numbering window. For example, if there are five points on a previous slide, the next slide should start with number six.

You can select custom bullets and numbers from the symbols' library (for example, tick boxes or archery targets) or even pictures from the Office.com art library. This menu also lets you adjust the size and colour of the bullets and numbers.

Other Basic Text Formatting Tools

The text formatting bar within the Home Ribbon tab contains a ton of options for text-tinkering. Before we move on, here are some more explanations of the basic formatting tools' functions.

- **Strikethrough**: To add a line through the middle of some text, select the text and hit the icon.

- **Change Case**: To turn a lower case word/sentence into upper case, or capitalize the first letter of each word in a title, use this drop-down menu.

- **Text Shadow**: This will give text a 3-D effect.

- **Character Spacing**: This can be handy when trying to make text fit into a box.

- **Line Spacing**: This drop-down menu in the Paragraph section on the Home tab allows you to select the gap between the lines of text within a particular content placeholder. The default setting is 1.0; double spacing, naturally, would be 2.0.

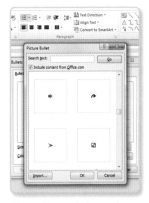

Above: Custom bullets and numbers can be found in the symbols' library or from the Office.com art library.

Hot Tip

Hitting the 'Clear All Formatting' button in Format tab (Mac) or in Paragraph section on the Home tab (PC) or using Control+Space (Command+Space) will clear the various bolds, underlines or colours from your text.

Above: There are many formatting functions available for text; all of these tools can be found in the text formatting bar in the Home tab.

FONTS

Fonts are the style in which your text is presented and there are literally thousands of them.

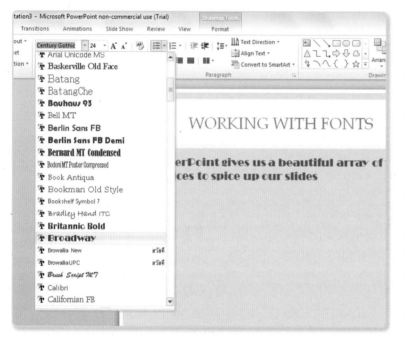

Above: There are almost countless fonts to choose from, all of which can be found in the drop down menu in the Home tab.

Changing Fonts

The easiest way to change the font of your text is to select the drop-down arrow from within the Ribbon. Hitting this will present the whole Fontbook available within Microsoft Office. If you choose one of these options while the relevant text is selected, it will instantly switch to the new font (PC only). To begin writing in a new font, make the selection when no text is selected and begin to type.

Hot Tip

If you know the name of the font you'd like to use, place your cursor in the font box that displays your current font and start typing. Once the name of your preferred font appears, hit Enter.

Text Fonts in Themes

If you have selected a theme for your PowerPoint presentation (see page 52) then it will include some pre-selected font pairings that work well together. For example, the Angles theme (shown in the screenshot left) works well

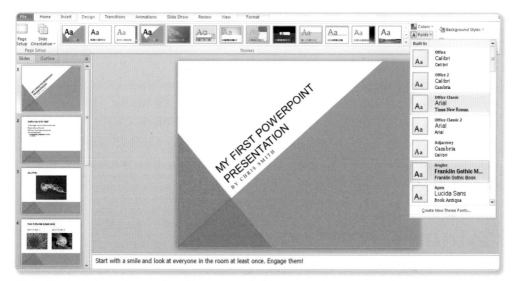

Above: Themes include some pre-selected font pairings which you can use for your chosen design.

with **Franklin Gothic Medium** for titles and Franklin Gothic Book for body text.

In order to borrow well-co-ordinated font pairings collated for the other themes, hit the Fonts drop-down menu in the Design tab to choose, for example, the Arial and Times New Roman pairing from the Office Theme.

Hot Tip

Like the colours within themes, these fonts have been chosen for a reason: they look good together. You're welcome to change them to your own combinations, but beware!

Replace Fonts

If you decide you want to abandon and replace a font that features prominently throughout your presentation, you can use the Replace tool within the Home tab. (Format > Replace Fonts on a Mac). Here you'll be presented with a dialogue box asking you to select a replacement from a drop-down menu.

COLOURS

Earlier in this book, we likened the process of building a PowerPoint presentation to decorating and furnishing an empty house. Unless you're living within the set of a Stanley Kubrick film, it's hard to imagine taking residence in a house with white painted walls and white furniture, so let's add a splash of colour to liven things up a little.

CHANGING FONT COLOURS

The default PowerPoint text colour is, naturally, black, but there's an entire spectrum of colours at our disposal here. The easiest way of changing your font colour is to select the drop-down arrow within the text formatting tools on the Home Ribbon tab, which presents the full range of options.

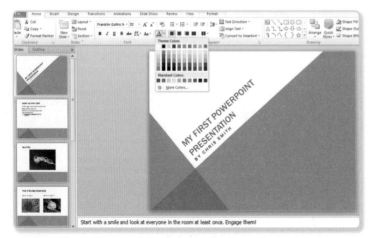

Above: The theme font colours list is great as it only gives you options that will co-ordinate with your selected theme.

Choosing Font Colours to Suit Your Theme

The first option when selecting from the drop-down menu is to select a font from within your theme colours. This is a helpful tool, as it only presents options that will co-ordinate with the overall look and theme you've selected for your presentation. As you can see, there are various shades to choose from for each theme colour; simply hover over the colour of your choice and click. If you've pre-selected the text you want to change, this will change the colour; otherwise, the next word you type will appear in the new hue.

Standard Colours

You're a rebel and you're not going to let Microsoft's highly-paid specialists inform your colour choice! As an alternative you can choose between the standard colours (the purest reds, blues, greens, etc.) that appear within the menu. Again, select the text first to change existing text.

The 'More Colors' Spectrum

The full rainbow of colours is available within this menu. You can drag your cursor around the wheel to select the most precise shade.

CHANGING THEME COLOURS

Once again, Microsoft's experts have put a lot of thought into selecting the colours for the

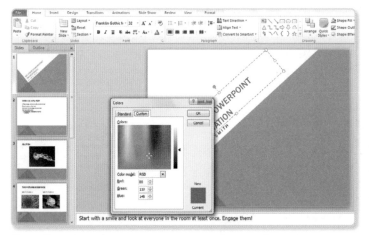

Above: The custom colour spectrum gives you complete control over your colour selection.

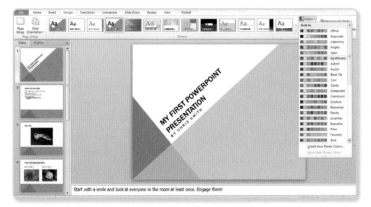

Above: You don't have to stick with the pre-selected colours of your chosen theme; you can select colourways from other themes to suit your presentation.

various theme designs and served up 12 different colours that match (text, backgrounds, boxes, hyperlinks and various design elements).

If you've chosen one theme but like the colour scheme from another, you can borrow it and apply it to your design. In order to achieve this, select the Colors option from the Design tab within the Ribbon (Themes on Mac) and choose from the drop-down menu. You'll see the names of the other themes next to the colour palette they employ.

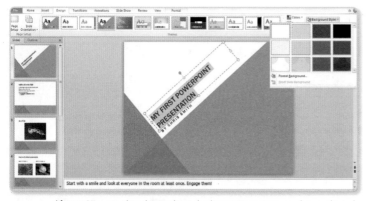

Above: You can alter the gradient shading options once you have selected your theme. This is easily done by the format background option in the Background Styles button.

CHANGING BACKGROUND COLOURS

As previously hinted, each PowerPoint theme has pre-defined background styles that appear behind all the content but also match up with the other design elements. Think of them as the wallpaper behind the paintings you hang on the wall. Each theme has 12 different styles, including solid colours and various gradient shading options (which neatly intersperse two or more colours).

Customizing Your Background Styles

The default PowerPoint Background Styles are attractive, but you can tailor them more to your own desires with the

Hot Tip

For beginners and experienced users alike, it's best to stay within the background colours indicated by your theme to avoid nasty colour clashes.

Format Background window within the Background buttons; here are some of the key options on offer.

- **Solid fill**: Paints the background with a single solid colour.

- **Gradient fill**: Allows you to customize the type, direction, colour, brightness and transparency of the gradient shading. Play with this and you'll get a feel for it.

- **Picture or texture fill**: Use this option to add a photo or pattern from your computer. Be careful, though: if there's too much going on within the frame, it'll be harder for your audience to see the important information clearly.

OLDER VERSIONS? In PowerPoint 2003, you can select Format > Background to access the same tools.

Hot Tip

If you're unhappy with the custom changes you've made to a background, you can simply hit the Reset Slide Background button to return it to the original settings (PC only).[EHT]

WORKING WITH WORDART AND TEXT STYLES

Once you're happy with your fonts, you can take it to the next level through Microsoft's WordArt Styles (Text Styles on Macs). Here you can furnish your words with a host of pre-set designs that add colour, outlines, gradient shading shadows and effects to your text, while still retaining your

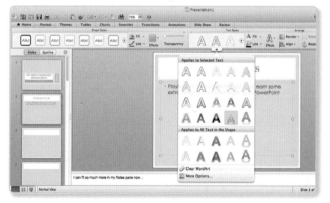

Above: WordArt styles provide an array of options that you can apply to individual words and letters or to everything within your content placeholder.

Hot Tip

Play around with the many WordArt styles by hovering over the various options within the drop-down menu. The text will change dynamically as you move your mouse. This way, you'll see what looks good and bad on your slides (PC only).

font. You can access the WordArt/Text Styles options through the Format tab, which only appears when working with text.

You can see three examples of the letter 'A' within the WordArt Styles pane, but select the drop-down arrow to bring up the full array of text styles.

You can choose to apply the text effects to everything within the content placeholder or just to the words you've highlighted.

OLDER VERSIONS? In PowerPoint 2003, select the WordArt box (a 3-D 'A') from the bottom toolbar to format text.

Text Fill and Text Outline

You can further customize text styles by using the following commands, which are located next to the WordArt Styles pane in the Format tab.

Above: You can easily change the colour of your text outline, providing a contrast with the fill or simply making it stand out.

↪ **Text Fill:** This will change the colour of the body of the text. You can select colours that match your theme or standard colours. If you'd just like an outline with no colour fill, select No Fill.

↪ **Text Outline:** This will change the colour of the outline of the text. If you don't want a text outline, it's easy to select No Outline.

Text Effects

These options, which appear within the Drawing pane of the Format tab in a drop-down menu beneath the Text Fill and Text Outline menus, take text design to the ultimate level.

- **Shadow:** Add a shadow beneath the text to suggest that light is shining on the words.

- **Reflection:** This option offers a slight reflection beneath the text.

- **Glow:** This effect gives the text a warm glowing outline.

- **Bevel:** A 3-D-like effect

- **3-D Rotation:** Toggling these settings will alter the angle of the text in 3-D space.

- **Transform:** Completely alters the shape of the text. For example, it can form a semi-circle, or it can be slanted up or down. Just hovering over the examples will show you how the effect will look on the slide (PC only).

Above: You can quickly and easily play with your text to transform its shape, shadow, reflection and glow!

Hot Tip

Rather than converting existing text to WordArt, you can insert a WordArt text box featuring your chosen text style. Hit the Insert tab (select Insert in top menu on Mac) and click the WordArt button; then click the style of your choice from the drop-down menu and a text box will appear in the centre of the slide with the default 'Your Text Here'. Overwrite it to add your own text in WordArt.

TRANSITIONS AND ANIMATIONS

We'll now move on to improving how your presentation looks when moving between information and between slides – transitions and animations are key to this.

TRANSITIONS

Transitions are attractive effects that can be employed to control how you move from slide to slide when you're delivering your presentation to an audience. They do not affect the information or how it appears within the slide but simply determine how one slide disappears and the next one appears. In order to access the Transitions control panel, you can select the dedicated Transitions tab within the PowerPoint Ribbon.

Types of Transition

Once you've selected the Transitions tab, you'll see the array of effects available to you. However, clicking the drop-down arrow will reveal the full extent, split into three categories.

- **Subtle**: Among these options are the more basic – but often most effective – transitions, such as Cut (jumps from one to the next) and Fade (adds a dissolve effect between slides).

- **Exciting**: Among the more elaborate transitions are the Honeycomb, Glitter and Vortex .

Hot Tip

In order to apply the transition settings you've chosen to the entire presentation, hit the 'Apply To All' button on the right of the Transitions tab.

- **Dynamic Content**: The text appears to land on the slide from a different location.

How to Add Transitions

Use Slide View on the left of the Window and select which slide you'd like to apply the transition to. Note that you will need to select the slide that will receive the transition, rather than the slide from which you'll be transitioning.

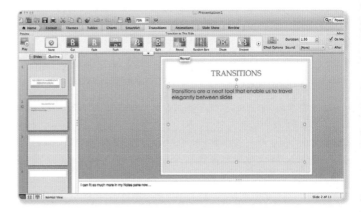

Above: The transitions menu (accessed as a tab for PC) provides an array of effect options to get your presentation moving (quite literally!).

Then, from the Transitions tab within the Ribbon, click the effect of your choice to apply it automatically to the slide. PowerPoint will then show you a representation of how it looks; in order to see it again, click the Preview button on the left of the tab. If you decide to change the transition, simply click on another one from the menu, whereas to delete a transition, click the 'None' icon from the drop-down menu.

OLDER VERSIONS? In PowerPoint 2003, hit the Slide Show menu and select Slide Transitions for a pop-up tab where you can choose from the various transition options.

Transition Options

Apart from adding the transition, you can also customize the direction in which it moves, its duration, any audio effects you'd like to add and how to advance, whether you'd like a sound to play alongside the transition.

- **Effect Options**: Here you can choose how the transition appears. For example, if you've selected the Shape option, you can choose whether the new slide transition appears as a square, diamond or circle and whether the shape moves in or out.

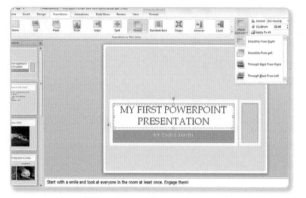

Above: Effect Options allow you to control transition timings, directions and sounds.

Right: The star symbol will appear next to your slide thumbnail once a transition has been applied.

Duration: Adjusting the numbers within this box will alter how drawn-out the transition is. You could build anticipation to a particular slide by making this 3–4 seconds long. Normally one second will suffice.

Sound: Here you can add stock sound effects to accompany the transition: a round of applause, perhaps? Want rid of the sound? Click No Sound within the drop-down menu.

Previewing Your Transitions

Applying a transition will automatically show you a preview of how it will look. Just click the Preview button on the left of the Transitions tab to play it again or to test duration and sound effects.

ANIMATIONS

Animations can control how information enters, moves within and exits a PowerPoint slide, and multiple animations can be added to each content placeholder. Animations can be applied to any object within a slide, from singular pieces to entire blocks of information.

Hot Tip

When a transition is applied, you'll also see a small box with an arrow next to the slide in Slide View or Slide Sorter View.

They are especially important when you wish to reveal your points one at a time or would like them to appear in a certain order. Like transitions, animations are also a very useful tool in improving the overall look and feel of your presentation. Animations have their own tab within the Ribbon user interface and selecting this tab will present all of the options available to you.

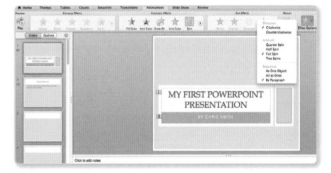

Above: The Animations tab controls the movement of the information you have chosen to animate. The star symbols indicate what kinds of animations are available.

Applying an Animation

In order to choose an animation, start by clicking on the Animations tab in the PowerPoint Ribbon user interface and then select the content placeholder featuring the information you'd like to animate. Choose whether you want an Entrance, Emphasis or Exit animation from the drop-down menu and click it to apply. This will instantly launch a preview of the effect you've chosen.

OLDER VERSIONS? Select Slide Show and Animation Schemes in PowerPoint 2003 to summon the animation options.

Types of Animation

Within the Animations tab, you'll see the star icons represent the various effects.

Hot Tip

If you want to apply the animation to a word/line/sentence of text, highlight it first, otherwise the animation will apply to the whole box.

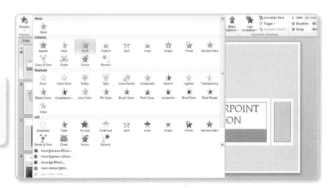

Above: The animation drop-down menu gives a vast range of options for the entrance, emphasis or exit of your information.

Pictured initially are the most commonly used tools, such as Appear (brings the text on screen with little fuss), Fly In, Fade and Wipe (bring the information in with slide design effects befitting their name). Selecting the drop-down arrow will reveal the full extent of the animations available and they are split into three 'E's. Mac users will see the three 'E's neatly contained within the Animations Ribbon tab.

Entrance: These animations allow your words to Fly, Float, Bounce, Swivel and more. These effects are colour-coded in green.

Emphasis: An emphasis effect can make your text or shape Pulse, Teeter, Spin and more. Emphasis effects are colour-coded in yellow.

Above: The Animations tab consists of a range of star icons, each representing available animations.

Exit: These animations perform the opposite action to the Entrance ones: instead of Appear, you have Disappear and instead of Fly In, you have Fly Out. The Exit effects are represented in red.

The Animation Painter Tool

Once you've added the animation, select the object and you'll see the Animation Painter button light up in the Advanced Animation Pane. Click it and your cursor will become a paintbrush; click within other placeholders to apply that animation to the new object.

Above: The animation painter tool turns your cursor into a paintbrush that allows you to quickly apply the same animation to other objects.

Using Motion Path

We have listed this option outside of the three 'E's (Entrance, Emphasis, Exit) because the Motion Path can be tailored to act like all three. It creates a pre-set path along which the object (text, picture, etc.) moves within the slide. So, if the Motion Path starts outside the slide and ends up within it, it's almost like an Entrance effect.

You'll see from the drop-down Animations menu within the Animation tab that Microsoft has kindly added some pre-set arcs, shapes, loops, lines and turns; select one to add it to your content placeholder. From there, you'll see a dotted line indicating the path along which the object will move. The green arrow represents the start and the red arrow represents the end of the path. We've selected the 'Arcs' tool, as you can see in the screenshot to the right.

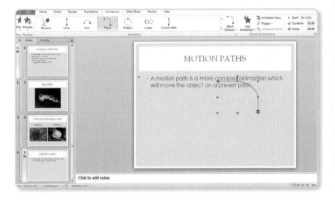

Above: The Motion Path tool works to combine the three 'E's (Entrance, Emphasis, Exit). It creates a pre-set path for the animation, and there is a range of path shapes to choose from.

These lines can be stretched/reversed or moved by clicking on them. In order to move the box to a new position, just grab it or use the markers to change its appearance. The effectiveness of Motion Paths can be quite hit-and-miss so it's best to play with them and see what you think looks good.

OLDER VERSIONS? In PowerPoint 2003, select Slide Show > Custom Animations and then under the Add Effect Menu, select the Entrance Emphasis, Exit and Motion path options.

Drawing a Custom Path

If you're feeling up to it, you can write your own Motion Paths by using the Custom Path tool within the Animations drop-down menu on the PC, or press the Motion Paths button on the

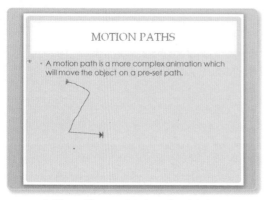

Above: If you want to be really original you can create a custom motion path, tailored to your presenting needs.

Animation tab (Mac). After you've selected your chosen text or object, choosing Custom Path will bring up the pen tool. Hold down your left mouse button and move the mouse/trackpad to draw. Double-click when you have finished and hit the Preview button to take a look.

Applying Multiple Animations

If you're so inclined, you can add an entrance animation, an emphasis animation *and* an exit animation to a single piece of information to create a combination of stylish effects.

In order to showcase how this works, we'll concentrate on adding them to a Title placeholder. First of all, add an entrance effect (we'll go with Fly In). Once you've added this, you'll see a number 1 box appear next to the title content placeholder.

Above: Applying multiple animations to one object isn't as tricky as it sounds. Each effect will show up on the left-hand edge of the slide so you can easily keep track of them.

In order to add a second effect (in our case the Pulse Emphasis), you'll need to use the Add Animation button within the Ribbon (if you select from the regular drop-down menu in the centre of the screen, PowerPoint will just overwrite your first selection on the PC).

Once you've selected the Emphasis, you'll see a number 2 box appear beneath the number 1 box on the left of the slide. In order to add a number 3, and an Exit animation, repeat the previous step. Now you should have an Entrance, Emphasis and Exit animation.

Using Effect Options

Just like the transitions we discussed previously, once you've selected an animation you can customize it further by using the Effect Options button. For example, if text is floating into a slide, you can use this tool to control whether it floats in from the top, bottom, left or right, or if you've selected Shapes from the Motion Paths animations, you'll be able to control exactly which shape you'd like to employ.

Using Effect Options to Customize Sequences

If you apply an animation to a content placeholder, PowerPoint will want to apply it to everything within the box, which means that, by default, everything will appear at once.

However, if you'd prefer your talking points to appear one at a time – which is great for bullet-pointed lists or when you're looking for feedback from your audience before revealing the next piece of information – then select the Effect Options from the Animations Ribbon tab and move down to Sequence. This will allow you to select whether the animation appears As One Object, All at Once or By Paragraph, i.e. there's a click needed to progress to the next point.

Hot Tip

When testing various animations, you can press the Preview button on the left of the Ribbon to see if you're happy with them.

Above: Animation Effect Options give you complete control over the look and movement of your animation from start to finish.

Above: If you want parts of information within one content placeholder to appear at different times you can use the Sequence tool, under the Effect Options button.

Hot Tip

Mac users need to access the Animation Pane in a roundabout way: hit View > Toolbox > Custom Animation.

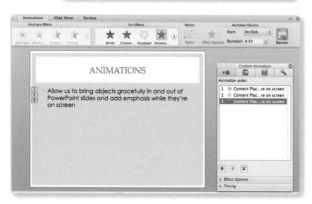

Above: The Advanced Animation Pane helps you to keep track of your animations and it's useful to always have this window open when working on animations.

Above: The trigger tool allows you to select a certain area of the slide to act as a trigger for beginning an animation.

THE ANIMATION PANE

Things can get a little complicated when working with animations: they're heavily customizable, there's a lot going on and a lot to consider. Thankfully, the PowerPoint Animation Pane can help to keep everything manageable.

It features the animations you've applied, the order in which they'll appear and the duration of the effect. When working with animations, it's wise to bring this up immediately; to do so, click the Animation Pane button within the Ribbon tab

Animation Triggers (PC only)

Once again, this is one of the more Advanced Animation settings; should you choose to, you can set up an effect to work when you click a certain area of the slide.

This is useful if you reach a certain spot in your presentation where you want to add emphasis to a particular point. In order to activate it, click the Trigger lightning bolt and select the object you'd like to use as the trigger (usually a placeholder or picture).

Reordering Animations

When working within PowerPoint, we don't always add the effects in the order we want them to appear. Thankfully, the Animation Pane can rectify that: once you've completed the addition process, grab the individual animations with your mouse (hold down the left mouse button) and move them further up or down the list. You can also click the Reorder Animation buttons to move them up and down.

Animation Timings Pane

Although, for the most part, your animations will be activated by a click of the mouse or by hitting the down arrow on your keyboard during a presentation, if you're going hands-free, you can add some manual timings to your animations.

The Timings pane within the Animation tab controls when your animations start, how long they'll last and how long it takes for them to appear. These settings are called Start, Duration and Delay. From this portion of the user interface, you can also control in which order the animations appear.

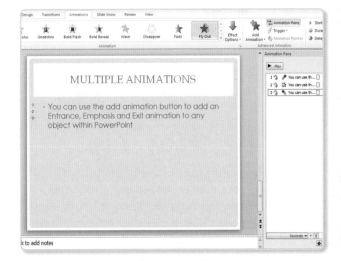

Above: The animation pane allows you to grab your animations and drag them to the order in which you want them to appear.

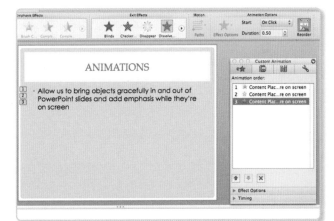

Above: The timings pane lets you control when your animations begin to appear and how long they will last for.

Starting an Animation

Selecting from the drop-down Start menu will allow you to choose if the animation commences with a click of the mouse (On Click), alongside the previous animation (With Previous) or following an animation (After Previous).

Hot Tip

To control the durations you can also click the orange shaded box within the Animation Pane and move it left or right, although this can be a bit fiddly at times. It's easier to double-click the box and adjust the settings in the pop-up window. (PC only).

Controlling the Duration of an Animation

In order to adjust the speed at which your animation moves, select the animation of your choice from the Animation Pane or click the corresponding number box within the main slide. Then you can choose the Duration tab within the Timing box in the Ribbon (the default is 0.5 seconds).

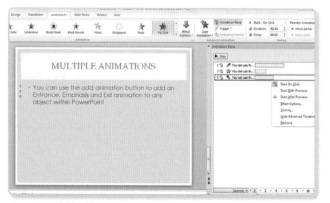

Above: The Animation Pane button also allows you to control the delay between several different animations.

Delaying an Animation

Within the Timing pane you can opt to delay the commencement of an animation. Mac users can access this functionality by selecting the Reorder button within the Animations tab. Within the Timing section you'll see the option to delay the start of the animation. For example, adding 1 second into the timing box next to 'Delay' will mean that there is a one-second gap between the end of one animation and the beginning of the next. You can see the timeline within the Animation Pane, pictured left.

EDITING SLIDES

Before we move on to creating our own custom slides, here are some basic tips on editing the existing PowerPoint slide designs.

MOVING CONTENT PLACEHOLDERS

Most of the time, those placeholders within Slide Layouts are perfectly positioned and aligned for our needs, but it's quite simple to move the boxes. Firstly, click the placeholder of your choice, hover your mouse over one of the outlines until the pointer becomes a four-headed arrow, and then hold down the mouse button and drag it to the new position.

RESIZING CONTENT PLACEHOLDERS

If you'd like to make the placeholder larger or smaller within the slide, in order to add another item (*see* page 128), then hover your mouse over one of the square or circular dots at the edges of the box. The cursor will then transform into a two-headed arrow icon; from there you can drag the shape in or out to make it bigger or smaller.

Above: It's very simple to resize your content placeholder to fit the design of each slide.

Hot Tip

Holding down Control while resizing keeps the centre of the object in the same place.

Above: Create content placeholders by selecting Content Placeholder from within the Text Box section of the Insert tab.

Above: Notes and Handouts also appear in the pop-up Header and Footer window. The same options apply but you can also add a header.

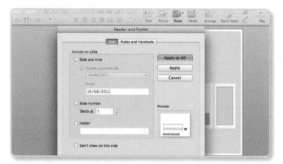

Above: You will find the Header & Footer button in the Insert tab on Ribbon for PC and on the insert section of the Home tab for Mac. This will summon a pop-up window.

CREATING CONTENT PLACEHOLDERS

If you're looking to add new content placeholders to blank slides or those already populated by content, you'll need to create them. To do this, click the Insert tab in the Ribbon and hit Content Placeholder within the Text box (on Mac hit Insert > Text Box) and the cursor will become an upside-down crucifix. You can then hold down the left mouse button and move the mouse/trackpad to begin creating the shape.

ADDING HEADERS AND FOOTERS

In order to add footers, you need to hit the Header & Footer button from the Insert tab in the Ribbon (Mac users select Insert Headers > Headers and Footers). This will summon a pop-up window offering date and time, slide number and text footer options. From here you can hit Apply to All or just Apply to add to the slide in question.

Headers and Footers in Notes and Handouts

You may notice the tab for Notes and Handouts within the pop-up Header and Footer window. All of the same options apply (page number, footer, date and time) but you can also add a header.

SLIDE MASTERS

Now that we're getting into the nitty-gritty of slide design and customization, it's time to call up the Slide Master tool and get creative.

WHAT IS A SLIDE MASTER?

A Slide Master, as the name suggests, is the key slide on which the others are based. So, if you modify the fonts, theme colour scheme, effects, backgrounds and placeholder sizes in the Slide Master then these changes will apply to each of the Slide Layouts (see page 62) within your theme.

Each presentation has three Slide Masters, whether you modify them or not. One for the presentation slides, one for the handouts and one for the notes page. The Slide Master tool might seem a little intimidating, but it's actually incredibly helpful and can save you lots of time when designing a presentation, as it keeps a host of design elements consistent throughout without changing each and every slide. Let's dig in.

THE SLIDE MASTER VIEW

In order to access the Slide Master tab tool, select the Slide Master button within the View tab in the Ribbon (alternatively, hold Shift and click the Normal View in the Status Bar). Mac users can press the View menu and move the mouse down to Masters before selecting Slide Masters (alternatively, select 'Edit Masters' within the Themes tab). Once you've done this, you'll notice a new tab that wasn't there before, next to the File tab (see screenshot on page130).

Accessing the Slide Master tool changes the Slide View tool to showcase the Slide Master at the top, and underneath are thumbnails of each of the different Slide Layouts within a certain theme. You'll also see an entirely new set of formatting tools within the Ribbon which will be described later in this section.

OLDER VERSIONS? In PowerPoint 2003 you'll find the Slide Master view within View > Master > Slide Master. There's also a pop-up toolbar to help you.

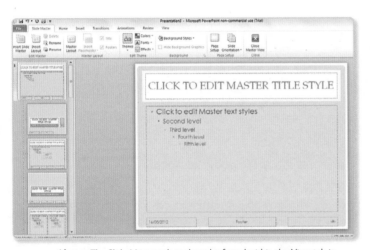

Above: The Slide Master tab tool can be found within the View tab in Ribbon for PC, and in the view menu, under Masters for Mac users.

WHAT'S IN A SLIDE MASTER?

The Slide Master features a content placeholder for the Master title style and one for the Master text style, along with the various paragraph levels (*see* page 90). It'll also feature any design information from the theme and the background style associated with it. If you've added a header and footer then they will also be apparent within this slide.

EDITING YOUR SLIDE MASTER

Any changes you make to the Slide Master (which is the number one slide you'll see in the Slide Master view) will apply to the rest of the slides in the

Hot Tip

It's a good idea to make the changes before adding all of the content to your remaining slides to ensure that nothing is knocked out of sync.

presentation *and* to those that you'll add to the presentation beyond that.

The process of editing the Slide Master is really no different to the changes we made to the fonts, format, colour and size when designing and editing the presentation in the first place. You can still use all of the shortcuts we mentioned earlier in the chapter (for example, Control+B, Control+U and Control+Shift+>) and you can right-click or click the Insert tab to access the full text-formatting panel. Once you're happy with your changes, you can select the Close Master View button to return to Normal View.

Above: There are lots of Theme options within Slide Master, allowing you to alter the setup of placeholders as well as colours, fonts and designs.

Hot Tip

When editing in Slide Master view, make sure that the Slide Master is selected rather than one of the layouts underneath, as changes to a Slide Layout will not be reflected in the Slide Master.

Editing the Theme Within the Slide Master View (PC only)

There are also options to change the themes, colours, fonts, text effects and background styles associated with that theme. Additionally, you can move, resize or delete the placeholders, as well as changing the page set-up (4:3, 16:9, etc.) and the orientation of your slides (portrait or landscape).

Adding Recurring Text and Objects to a Master Slide

You may want to add an item that appears in every slide throughout your presentation; perhaps you'd like to include a self-portrait, a shape, icon or a consistent text mantra you want your audience to take from the presentation. You can do this by selecting the Insert tab while in Slide Master View and draw the object of your choice (Mac users select the object from the Insert pane within the Home tab).

Above: You can add additional Slide Masters to your project, which can be saved and then selected from the Custom Design Option.

Adding Another Slide Master

It's possible to add more than one Slide Master to each PowerPoint project; this will give you the opportunity to create more custom design options for your presentation. Click Insert Slide Master from the Slide Master tab in the Ribbon and this will add a clean Slide Master beneath the existing one, complete with each Slide Layout associated with that. Make your changes within this series and then return to Normal View. Now, next time you add a New Slide to a presentation you'll be able to select from the Custom Design option.

> # Hot Tip
>
> **Ensure you place the recurring object somewhere in the design where it won't interfere with the other information in the slide layout.**

Left: You can add additional Slide Masters to your project, which can be saved and them selected from the Custom Design Option.

Hot Tip

If you make use of the Edit Theme pane while working within Master Slide Layouts then the whole presentation will be affected.

EDITING MASTER SLIDE LAYOUTS

At various points during this section we've mentioned that, as well as editing the Master Slide, you can also edit the individual Slide Layouts within a theme. Changes to text, titles and placeholders will not affect the whole presentation but will apply to that particular layout, each time you use it in your presentation. Each of the editing tools we mentioned in the Editing Slide Master section (see page 130) are also available to you when editing Master Slide Layouts.

OLDER VERSIONS? There's no opportunity to edit layouts within PowerPoint 2003 – just the Title Slide and Title and Content Slide.

Creating New Slide Layouts

Microsoft has done a fine job of creating the various Slide Layouts that are present within each of the PowerPoint themes. However, you can tear up the playbook and create your own to save and use consistently throughout your presentation.

In order to enable this feature, hit View > Slide Master > Insert Layout. This

CLICK TO EDIT MASTER TITLE STYLE

Above: Slide Master allows you to create and insert new custom layouts which you can save and use throughout your presentation.

will summon a relatively blank canvas, featuring the chosen theme design, a title content placeholder and the footers (both of which can be dispensed with by deselecting the boxes in the Master Layout pane). It will appear at the bottom of the Slide View pane but will populate the Current Slide view.

Click the Insert Placeholder drop-down menu within Master Layout in order to choose the style of placeholder you wish to add. You can also use the Insert tab (this appears within the Home tab on Macs) to draw shapes (something described in more detail in the next chapter). Once you've finished perfecting your design, click Rename within the Edit Master pane to save it. After returning to Normal View and hitting New Slide, you'll see this layout featured within the drop-down menu.

Saving Your Master Slides as a Custom Template

Way back in Chapter two we mentioned that when creating a presentation from a template (see page 54), there was a little section called My Templates, reserved for your own creations.

At that point we didn't have any, but now we do. In order to save your newly fashioned Slide Masters as a Custom Template, select Save As from the File tab, hit the drop-down menu, click on PowerPoint Template (.potx) and hit save. The saved template will now appear to you in My Templates in the New section of the Backstage View.

Right: Handouts Master allows you to control the Page Setup, Handout Orientation, Slide orientation (PC only) and Slides Per Page and Placeholders.

CHANGING THE HANDOUT AND NOTES MASTERS

Earlier in the chapter we mentioned that there are at least three Masters for each PowerPoint presentation we create: beyond the Slide Masters you add, there are Notes and Handout Masters, which you can also tailor to your own needs.

Creating a Custom Handout Master

Select View and then Handout Master (use View > Masters > Handout Masters on a Mac) to summon the Handout Master tab, which will appear next to the File tab. From this view you can tailor the Page Setup, Handout Orientation, Slide Orientation (PC only), Slides Per Page, as well as Placeholders like Header, Footer, Date and Page Number.

There is, however, no opportunity to edit the size of the slides represented within the Handout View.

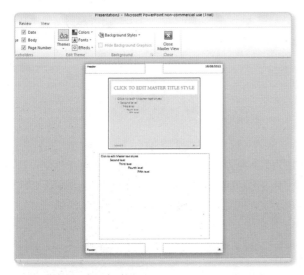

Above: You can customize the Notes Master to your needs, allowing you to amend the set-up and orientation of notes on your slides.

Creating a Custom Notes Master

Once again, hit View > Notes Master (Themes > Edit Master > Notes Master on Macs) to access this page. From here you can amend the set-up, orientation of the notes and the orientation of the slides appearing on the page (PC only). Additionally, you can customize what appears on the Notes page and change the sizes of the slide representation and the notes placeholder in the same way you'd alter the size of a content placeholder.

ADDING TO A PRESENTATION

ADDING IMAGES

Adding photographs or Clip Art is a great way to spice up your slide show, while PowerPoint is also a great tool for creating beautiful photo albums. In this section, we'll show you how to break up the tedium of text-based slides.

Above: Within each content placeholder there are icons indicating objects that you can insert.

ADDING PICTURES

Helpfully, within every content placeholder, there are six icons that allow you to insert content (tables, charts, video, etc.). One of those buttons features a photograph and the message 'Insert photo from file'. Selecting this icon will allow you to choose a photo from File (stored on your computer). You can also hit the Insert tab and then the Picture button to achieve this.

Both actions will summon the Insert Picture dialogue box. Find the picture that you'd like to use and press Open. The photo will now appear within the content placeholder.

OLDER VERSIONS? In PowerPoint 2003 photos and Clip Art can be added using the Insert menu or the toolbar at the foot of the Window.

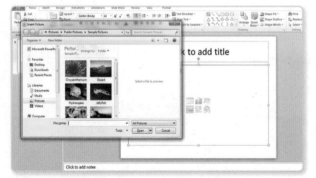

Above: Simply select the picture you would like to use when the box appears and press Open.

Adding Pictures Outside of Content Boxes

If you'd like your picture to appear within a particular content placeholder, it's important to use the Insert tool within the placeholder or to select the placeholder before you use the Insert tool from the Ribbon.

If you don't do this – or if you're using a blank slide layout – the photograph will just appear in the centre of the slide. If the photo you've chosen is larger than the confines of the slide, it will be scaled to fit.

Image File Formats

File formats are represented by the letters that appear after the dot in the file name (for example, .jpg, .tiff and .bmp). Since PowerPoint is such a universal tool, it'll play nicely with most formats.

Above: If you insert a picture within the content placeholder, which would otherwise be larger than the slide, it will be automatically scaled to fit.

ADDING CLIP ART

Microsoft has given us a sizable library of stock photos to kit out our PowerPoint presentations. These images and illustrations are called Clip Art. Just like Pictures, there's an Insert Clip Art button within all content placeholders. Click it to open the Clip Art pane on the right side of the PowerPoint Window (Media Browser on Mac).

Use the 'Search for' bar to type in the type of picture you'd like to use (we typed in 'Love') and hit Go to bring up the available photos. You can narrow down the types of media file results by ticking or deselecting Photographs, Illustrations, Videos and Audio from the drop-down 'Results should be' menu. Click the image once and the placeholder will adopt the Clip Art.

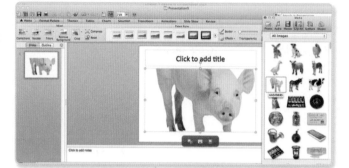

Above: Clip Art has a great library of images that you can use to embellish your presentation.

For Mac users it's a little trickier as there's no search box to refine the items within the clip art section of the Media Browser. You'll need to choose categories from the drop-down menu in the Media Browser and then drag the item to the relevant placeholder.

Adjusting the Size, Repositioning and Rotating Your Picture

Once you've added the picture, be it to a placeholder or to the slide itself, it's easy to resize, reposition and rotate it to your own specifications.

- **Resize to scale:** To resize the picture and keep the scale, click and drag one of the circular indicators at the edges of the photo.

- **Freeform resize:** Use the square indicators across the top and bottom of the object to adjust height or width.

- **Repositioning:** To move the photo elsewhere on your slide, select the picture and drag it to the preferred position within the slide.

Above: Once you have selected and placed your image you can alter and adjust the size, position and rotation.

Rotating: You'll see a green circle above the object. Click and drag it clockwise or anticlockwise to rotate the picture. In order to rotate a picture in 90-degree increments, use the Rotate menu within the Arrange pane.

Changing the Size Using the Format Tab

Clicking on a picture will automatically summon the Format tab in the Ribbon. Some of the options that appear within this tab are as follows:

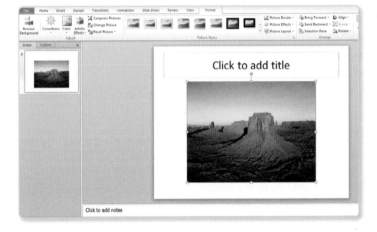

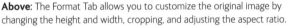

Above: The Format Tab allows you to customize the original image by changing the height and width, cropping, and adjusting the aspect ratio.

Shape height and shape width: Change the size of the picture by clicking the up and down arrows in the height and width boxes. The aspect ratio is automatically locked so increasing the height will also increase the width accordingly. On Macs make sure there's a tick in the Lock Aspect Ratio box in the Size panel. You can also type in the size of your choice.

Crop: By hitting the crop button in the Size pane will summon black borders at the corners of the picture. Use these to select the exact area of the photo you'd like to use and then hit the Crop button again to confirm.

Crop to Shape (Mask on Mac): You can turn the shape into a circle, rectangle, a speech bubble or even an equation symbol. The picture will maintain its look but will be cropped within the shape.

Hot Tip

In some instances, PowerPoint will not maintain the aspect ratio of your picture when dragging in the borders. To ensure that the proportions aremaintained, hold the Shift key.

Aspect Ratio: This tool crops the picture to fit the aspect ratio chosen.

Fill: Fill resizes the picture to fill the shape completely.

Fit: This option will show the entire photo within the dimensions of the placeholder, but it may not fill all areas.

See page 148 for on-screen resizing options for Mac users.

ADJUSTING AN IMAGE'S APPEARANCE

The Picture Tools Format tab features a pane called Adjust. Here you can ditch the background in the picture, make contrast and brightness corrections, add a colour scheme and apply filters with Artistic Effects. Many of these tools apply to videos and audio so remember them for later on in the chapter.

Removing the Background

Clicking Remove Background will launch PowerPoint's attempt to leave only the foreground in place by highlighting the areas to be deleted in purple. To accept the changes hit the Keep Changes' tick button, whereas to reject them, click 'Discard All Changes'.

In order to keep or delete more areas of background, select the Mark Areas to Keep/Remove buttons and click around the edges of the photo you'd like to keep/remove. Hopefully when you're finished, you'll have a perfectly tailored image of a tiger with no background information (see opposite page). For Mac users, after selecting Remove Background, the cursor will appear with a plus icon. Draw lines within

Hot Tip

Draw a straight line across the area of the image you'd like to keep and then fine tune with individual clicks in smaller areas that have been missed.

the picture, showcasing areas you'd like to keep and press Enter. To remove elements from the picture, hold the Command key to turn the plus into a minus and then draw lines in the same way.

Above: The Remove Background option will automatically remove the parts of the image that are not in the foreground; to be more precise you can manually select areas to delete and keep yourself.

Making Corrections to Images

The drop-down Corrections menu, within the Picture Tools Format tab, features a host of pre-set options for you to adjust the sharpness and softness and the brightness and contrast. As you can see from the screenshot (below), you can choose to soften or sharpen in increments of 25 per cent. It's a similar story with the Brightness and Contrast options. Top left will decrease both by 40 per cent and bottom right will increase both by 40 per cent, while the centre thumbnail is neutral. To tailor these options more precisely, select the Picture Correction Options at the bottom of the drop-down menu.

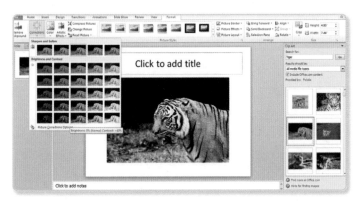

Above: The Corrections menu offers a large range of pre-set correction options.

Hot Tip

Select the 'More Variations' option at the foot of the drop-down Color menu to select a colour that matches your theme.

Making Colour Changes

From the drop-down Color menu (Recolor on Macs) within the Adjust tab, you can alter the Color Saturation (Color Tone on Macs) from no colour to a 400 per cent colour boost and the Tone from low to high temperature, while also Recoloring the picture completely. Hover over the various options to preview.

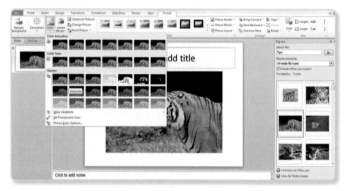

Above: The Color menu contains options for saturation levels as well as complete recolouring.

You can also click the Set Transparent Color option and then click a colour within the image that'll be completely see-through. However, you can only select one colour to be transparent (for Mac users it's a different story; see pages 148–149). For more precise Saturation, Tone and Recolor options, summon the Picture Color Options.

Adding Artistic Effects

Summon the drop-down Artistic Effects option to turn your photo into a pencil sketch or a painting, or to look like a watercolour painting or frosted glass window. This feature is called 'Filters' on Mac.

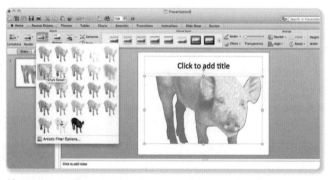

Above: Artistic Effects can give your pictures that extra edge; choose from a pencil sketch or watercolour painting, amongst many others.

Reset or Change (PC only)

Hit Change Picture to override the current snap from a file on your computer. Hit Reset Picture to delete all of the adjustments and effects you've made to a picture. Selecting the drop-down menu here will also allow you to reset any changes you've made to the size of the image and return it to its original state.

ADJUSTING THE STYLE

Click on the Picture Tools Format tab when working with an image you've added to a slide and you'll see the large Picture Styles pane packed with a bunch of framing options. Hover over these with a mouse to preview and click to select. More Picture Styles are available by selecting the drop-down arrow in the corner of the pane. From here you can add different shapes, edges and shadow effects.

Right: You can add a little depth to your slides by selecting effects such as the Beveled Oval for your images.

Picture Border and Picture Effect

These tools, within the Picture Styles pane, allow you to choose borders that adopt your theme's colours while the weight (i.e. thickness) of the border can also be determined from the menu.

Selecting from Picture Effects is similar to the WordArt settings for enhancing text (*see* page 113). Here you can also add Shadow, Glow, Reflection or a different perspective on how the image appears in 3-D space.

Picture Layout and SmartArt

Selecting from the drop-down Picture Layout menu also enables us to incorporate our pictures into SmartArt graphics. As we explained in

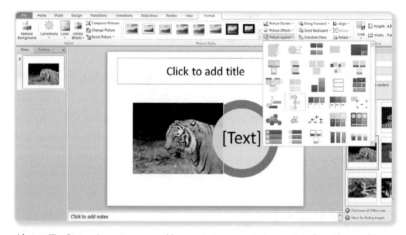

Above: The Picture Layout menu enables you to incorporate images into SmartArt graphics

Chapter one (*see* page 25), SmartArt turns pictures and words into design features that can break up endless bullet points.

In order to convert a picture to SmartArt (PC only), select a picture (click it) and hit Picture Layout from within the Picture Styles pane and select a diagram from the drop-down menu. For example, your picture could represent a bullet point in a SmartArt list or a thumbnail image to illustrate a related point (see the images above for some examples). We'll talk more about integrating images within SmartArt later in this section.

ARRANGING TEXT, IMAGES AND OBJECTS

If you're combining multiple images and words (or video, charts and tables), you may need to adjust how they're arranged so that, for example, text isn't hidden behind pictures.

Hit the Format tab for each content type (picture or text box) to add the Selection and Visibility pane to the right of the PowerPoint Window. From here, you can reorder the objects on the page (it's likely that you'll want the Content Placeholder at the top of this list). Be sure not to put dark pictures behind dark text, as it will obscure the visibility of your text.

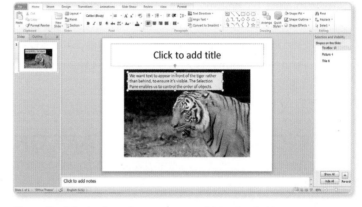

Above: The Selection Pane allows you to control the order of objects so that both your text and images are clearly visible.

Alternatively, to move individual objects back and forward within a slide, first you need to click on them. Then, using the Arrange pane from the Home tab, choose from the options Bring Forward, Bring To Front, Send Backwards or Send to Back. Mac users have a great tool at their disposal: see page 149.

> ## Hot Tip
> **Deselect the eye icons within the Selection and Visibility pane to see how your slides look with or without the various elements.**

Aligning Images or Objects

As with text-based placeholders, you can also anchor images to certain points of the page. Click an image and select the Align menu within the Arrange pane. Here you can snap the image to the left, right, centre, top, middle or bottom of the slide.

Grouping Images or Objects

Grouping together a series of images or objects (shapes, text, video, etc.) is useful, as it allows you to apply actions to them all at once (for example, rotating, flipping, moving or resizing). In order to group the objects, hold down the Control key and select each one; this should highlight them all. Then, in the Arrange Pane of the Format tab, hit Group. Images and objects can be grouped or ungrouped at any time.

PICTURES AND CLIP ART ON MAC

Here are some of the nuances that Mac users will notice when working with the Format Pictures tab in the Ribbon.

→ **Insert from Photo Browser:** This brings up the Media pane and allows you to select images from your iPhoto library, Facebook account (if it's linked to iPhoto) or PhotoStream (Apple's online storage solution). Once you've found the image of your choice, drag it into the content placeholder.

Above: The Photo Browser for Mac enables you to select images from a variety of sources.

- **Crop Tool**: Whenever you add an image, you'll see the on-slide crop tool which helps you to position/size it perfectly. The Crop, Fill and Fit settings are all present here (*see* pages 141–142).

- **Transparency**: PC users can only make one colour of an image transparent (*see* page 144), which doesn't make much sense. Mac users can make an entire image transparent using the slider within the Format Picture pane. Making an image transparent allows you to feature it prominently behind text, without obscuring your words.

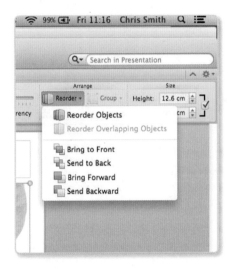

- **Arranging Slides**: An unique feature of PowerPoint on the Mac is Reorder Objects screen (*see* screenshot to right), which allows you to drag items manually to the foreground and background within a slide. Bring up this screen from the Reorder drop-down menu.

Above: The Recorder Objects screen for Mac allows you to drag items manually to the foreground and background.

IMAGES IN TEMPLATES

One of the key uses for PowerPoint in the home is to create photo slide shows of family occasions. As we've discussed in Chapter one (*see* page 54), there are pre-set PowerPoint templates which make this easy.

Hot Tip

When working with templates, don't use the Change Picture or Insert Picture options from the Ribbon to replace an existing photo in a placeholder. It may mess with the formatting of the template and the photos won't conform to the placeholder.

Above: You can use a pre-set PowerPoint template to create an interactive photo album and slide show

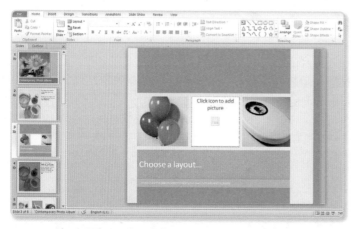

Above: When working with a pre-set photo album template you must begin by deleting the stock shots currently occupying the slots.

Select File > New > Sample Templates (Command+Shift+P > Templates > All on Mac) to choose from the Classic, Contemporary and Urban photo albums. We'll go with the Contemporary option, which you can see to the left.

In order to add your own photos to the various placeholders, you must first delete the stock shots currently occupying the slots. Click on the picture and press backspace to reveal the 'Insert Picture from File' icon in the placeholder. Click this to add a picture as you normally would, and it will conform to the size of the placeholder. Then use the image editing tools listed above to customize your photo.

CREATING A CUSTOM PHOTO ALBUM

PowerPoint 2007 and 2010 for PC feature a neat Photo Album creation tool that doesn't involve working with templates. The wizard will create a series of slides from a folder on your computer featuring the photos of your choice in the style of your choice – and here's how.

1. Select Photo Album from the Insert Images pane and click 'New Photo Album' to launch the wizard.

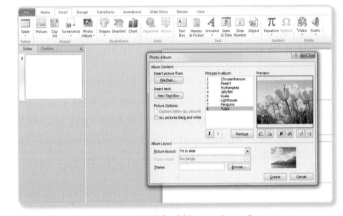

2. Click File/Disk to choose the picture(s) from your computer, then select them all and press Insert. All of the pictures are now listed in a numbered box, with a preview next door.

Above: PowerPoint 2007 and 2010 for PC have a photo album creation tool that doesn't involve working from a template; use the Wizard to select a folder of images and go from there.

3. From here you can add captions to all pictures or make them black and white by selecting the respective tick boxes. If you want you can click to add a text box next to the picture of your choice.

4, There are up/down arrows for moving pictures up and down in order of appearance; you can also remove individual pictures, use the rotate buttons and toggle with contrast and brightness.

The Album Layout section of the window allows you to determine how many pictures you'd like per page (the default is just one), the frame shape or even to pick from one of the PowerPoint themes. Once you're happy with everything, press Create and you'll have a quick and easy photo album. Now all you need to do is add text, titles and captions.

Hot Tip

Don't worry if you've missed out a picture; you can hit Photo Album > Edit Photo Album to add more snaps to your creation. To avoid having to do this, try to create a folder on your desktop featuring all of the pictures you'd like to use.

ADDING VIDEO AND AUDIO

Adding videos or audio from your computer or from the internet is a great way to add illuminating and entertaining content to your PowerPoint presentation – and it's just as easy as adding images. After explaining how to add audio and video separately, we'll talk about the playback and formatting tools together, as they're very similar.

ADDING VIDEO

Select the video reel icon within a content placeholder to add a video from file, which can be any video you have saved on your computer. Simply locate the video of your choice from the pop-up dialogue box and click Insert. The video will fit to the content placeholder as best it can or appear in the centre of the slide. You'll now see a Video Tools tab appear in the Ribbon with two sub-tabs: Format and Playback.

Above: Add a video by using the video reel icon within a content placeholder.

Video Browser on Mac

As with photos (and indeed audio, symbols and shapes), you can insert video using the handy Media Browser. In order to summon this, click the Insert Media button within the Home tab and select Movie Browser.

This browser has the added advantage of showing the clips at difference sizes (high, medium resolution, etc.) to enable you to keep the file size down. Once you've found the clip, just drag it into the slide.

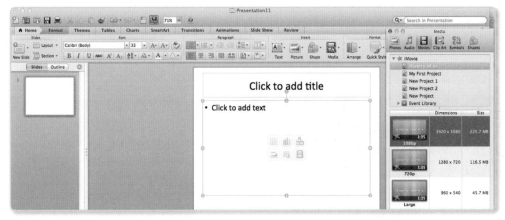

Above: For Mac users, locate the Media Browser from the Insert Media button within the Home tab.

Compatible Video File Formats

There are hundreds of different video codecs in the world and not all of them will work with PowerPoint. The following will cover most videos you shoot on your smartphone, video camera or have downloaded from the internet:

→ Windows Media file (.asf)
→ Windows Video File (.avi)
→ Movie File (.mpg or .mpeg)
→ Windows Media Video (.wmv).

Hot Tip

If the video lives on the computer on which you're going to be presenting, you can simply link to a video rather than embedding. Add a video as normal but before you click Insert, hit the arrow next to it and select Link to File instead. However, if you plan on sending or sharing your video you'll need to embed it using the Insert method to ensure it remains within the presentation.

ADDING VIDEO FROM SHARING WEBSITES (PC ONLY)

Luckily, PowerPoint doesn't limit you to adding videos to your own computer. It can also embed videos from sharing websites like YouTube, meaning that there are literally hundreds of millions of videos at your disposal. So, if you want to add suspense with the opening credits to Dr. Who, that's not a problem.

Above: Picture 1: Locate and copy the sharing code for your chosen video, from the online webpage.

Above: Picture 2: Under the Insert tab, click on video and select 'video from website'. In the dialogue box you will need to enter the sharing code.

Embed Codes

Any video sharing website which features embed codes (such as (www.funnyordie.com or www.dailymotion.com) can be inserted into your presentation:

1. Firstly, you'll need to be connected to the internet (when preparing and delivering the slideshow), then click the Video tab from the Insert tab and select Video from Web Site. This launches a dialogue box where you'll need to embed the code.

2. In order to obtain YouTube embed codes, point your web browser to www.youtube.com and find the video of your choice (see Picture 1). Then select the Share button beneath the video to reveal a new set of tools. Click embed, making sure you select the 'use old embed code' tick

box (the new embed code won't work), and copy that code (Control+A and then Control+C).

3. Go back to PowerPoint and paste the code into the dialogue box (Control+P), as in Picture 2. Click Insert and the video should appear on the slide or within the placeholder you selected. It'll just appear in black, but press the Play button in the Ribbon and it will play. These videos can be resized like any other video (Picture 3).

Hot Tip

If the Video from Web Site option is greyed-out then make sure you have the latest version of Adobe Flash installed on your PC (go to get.adobe.com/flashplayer for more details).

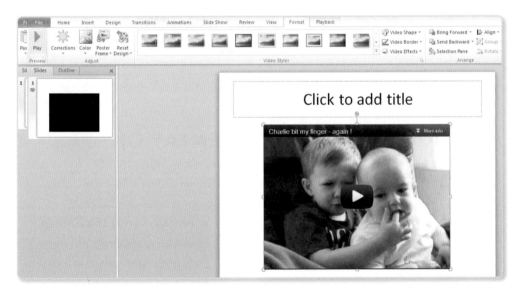

Above: Picture 3: Make sure you are connected to the internet when you give your presentation for the video to work!

ADD VIDEO FROM CLIP ART (PC ONLY)

Clip Art also features video in the form of short animated .gif files that can be added to slides. Select Insert > Video > Clip Art Video to narrow Clip Art selections down to videos and search (remember to tick 'Include Office.com content' for a wider selection); we searched for 'Dance'.

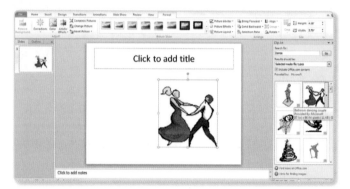

In order to preview the animation, right-click the arrow beside it and hit Preview/Properties. If you're happy with it, you can click to insert. Note that you'll only see the video/animation working within the slide when you're previewing or presenting the slideshow.

Above: You can also select short animated videos from the Clip Art folder; simply search for a keyword such as 'dance'.

AUDIO

In Chapter three (*see* page 118) we spoke of adding audio clips, such as a round of applause or a drum roll, to form a transition between slides, but the aural goodness in PowerPoint goes way beyond that. Here's how to add your favourite songs or sound effects to your slideshow.

ADDING AUDIO TO A PRESENTATION

Click the Audio icon from the Insert tab to add a clip from File. Select the clip of your choice from the pop-up dialogue box and hit Insert. It'll then appear within the slide, represented by a speaker icon and a playback menu that mirrors the video control panel explained in The On-slide Media Playback Controls (*see* page 158). Mac users can also use the Media Browser we mentioned on page 152 (Home tab > Media > Audio Browser).

Left: Add audio to your presentation by selecting the Audio icon from the Insert tab. This will enable you to select a track from your computer.

You can also select the Audio button from within the Insert tab to add sound from File, Clip Art and even make your own recordings.

ADDING AUDIO FROM CLIP ART (PC ONLY)

Clip Art also contains a host of .wav audio files you can apply to your presentation. Use Insert > Audio > Clip Art Audio to summon the Clip Art pane; tick 'Include Office.com content' to widen your options and add keywords to look for matches. If you've found a sound you like, just click to add it to your slide.

RECORDING YOUR OWN AUDIO

If none of the Clip Art sound effects or the tracks from your music library fit the bill, you can use your PC's or Mac's internal microphone to record sound. Select 'Record Audio' from the Insert Audio button and once you're ready to start warbling, press the red

Above: If you want to record your own audio clip, you can use the internal microphone of your Mac or PC to do so. Simply select 'Record Audio' from the Insert Audio button.

record button. Once you're done, press stop. Press play to preview it and if you're happy, hit OK to insert the sound. Mac users can select Insert > Audio > Record Audio to access the same functionality.

Compatible Audio File Formats

You'll be able to add any audio file you've copied from a CD and most files that you've downloaded from online stores like iTunes, Amazon, 7Digital or more. The list of compatible file formats is as follows: .mid (or .midi), mp3, .m4a, .mp4, .wav, .wma.

Hot Tip

You can check the file format of your audio clip, video or photo by right-clicking the file and selecting Properties (Info on Mac).

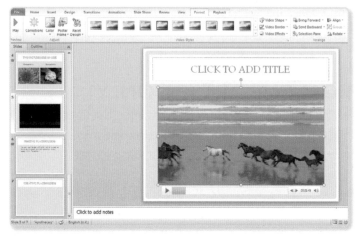

Above: The media controls allow you to start, stop, rewind and forward your clip.

ON-SLIDE MEDIA PLAYBACK CONTROLS

Whenever you add an audio or video clip, you'll see the media panel nestling beneath it. From here you can click the play button to start and stop (the space key also works), while using the rewind and forward options to browse through the clip at greater speed. The clock indicates how far you've progressed within the clip, while the speaker icon allows you to control the volume – just like the remote control on your home DVD player.

VIDEO AND AUDIO PLAYBACK TOOLS

Once you've added a clip, you'll see the Video/Audio Format and Video/Audio Playback tabs appear in the Ribbon. Select Playback to control the volume, and when (and from where) the clip starts, loops, fades, etc.

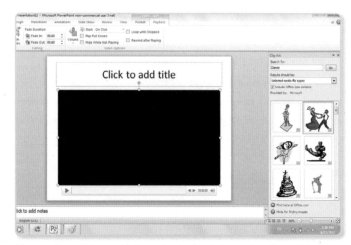

Above: When you have added a media clip the playback tab will appear in Ribbon, allowing you to control volume, looping, etc.

Adding a Poster Frame (Video Only)

Rather than having an unattractive black box on your video slide, you can add an image to your video to appear as a placeholder before you press play. Click the Poster Frame menu in the Format tab and you'll see you can select an image from file; alternatively, you can pause the video at the most apt moment and then hit Poster Frame > Current Frame. When you arrive at the slide, this is the image you'll see.

Add a Bookmark

Adding a bookmark or multiple bookmarks to your media clip enables you to anchor text or other objects to appear at certain points, by using the Animations tool. To select a bookmark, hit play and when the video/audio reaches the point of your choice click the Add Bookmark within the Playback tab and a white bubble will be added to the media progress meter.

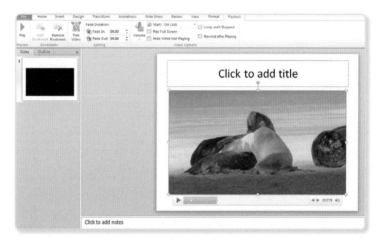

Above: You can add bookmarks in order to trigger animations, anchor text objects and more. To do this, play the media and hit the Add Bookmark button at the correct place within the media clip.

Then select another object within the slide and hit the Animations pane. Add your animation, select the text and then hit the Trigger button. You can then select 'Bookmark 1' and the text will fly, float or appear on the screen at the precise moment of your choosing.

Trimming Your Video or Audio (PC Only)

Once you've inserted the media file, hit Trim Video/Audio from within the Playback tab (PowerPoint 2010 for PC only) and you'll be presented with the window on the next page.

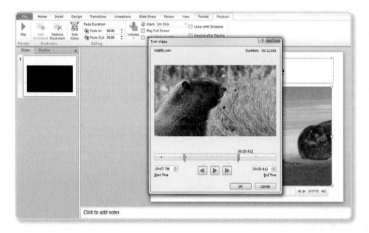

Above: Use the Trim Video/Audio button in the Playback tab to select where you would like the clip to start and stop.

Play the clip and then pause where you'd like it to start (if you know the time codes, you can just insert them into the relevant Start Time/End Time boxes) and then drag the green marker to the time marker. Do the same with the red marker at the end portion of the clip and click OK. You'll now see the newly trimmed clip within your slide. However, this can't be done with embedded clips from the internet.

Hot Tip

To add a little professional polish to your video or audio clip, use the Fade In/Fade Out tool and set both timers in the Playback tab to 0.5 seconds.

More Video and Audio Playback Options

The Options pane of the Playback tab (the Playback options drop-down on Mac) offers some more interesting tools for perfecting your use of media files.

○ **Volume**: Controls the loudness of your clip.

○ **Start**: Choose whether a click is required to start your video/audio or whether it'll begin automatically when you arrive at the slide.

○ **Play Full Screen (video only)**: Selecting this will allow the video to take over the entire slide while it is playing. Great if you have no other information to show alongside it.

○ **Loop until Stopped**: If you tick this box the clip will begin playing again from the start once it reaches the end. Press stop or hit the space bar to stop it. This is more useful for audio if you want the sound to play for the entire time that particular slide is displayed.

Rewind after Playing: Select this tick box if you plan on showing the clip more than once.

The Video Tools Format Tab

If you've added a movie from your computer you can edit it in the same way that you can edit a picture (see page 144), i.e. you can make the same Corrections and Color changes, while you'll also have access to the same Crop tools, Styles, Borders and Effects. Essentially, the entire Video Format (Movie format on the Mac) tab is much the same as the Picture Tools Format tab, so apply the same instructions listed earlier in the chapter to customize your video even further.

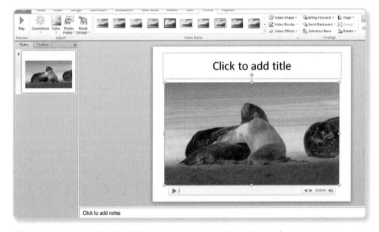

Above: Using the Video Tools Format Tab you can edit a video in the same way you can edit a picture; experiment with colour corrections, cropping, styles and effects.

Formatting the Audio Clip

There's not much you'll need to do within the Audio Tools Format tab (Audio Format on Mac). There's no real need to alter the appearance of the speaker icon, which appears on the presentation. You may like to use the size arrows to increase the size or you may like to click the 'Hide During Show' tick box so the icon isn't visible on the slide, but aside from that, move along – nothing to see here.

TABLES

Tables are useful in PowerPoint presentations when you're seeking to present figures and information in an easily comparable format. If you run a local bowling league you can easy match up the names of players with the numbers of games played, wins, losses, strikes, gutterballs and points. If you're presenting the results of a poll, you can add the question and the proportion of recipients who selected each answer. Like most things within PowerPoint, tables are easy to create and can be richly designed and customized.

ADDING A TABLE

You can incorporate a table into an existing context placeholder by simply selecting Insert Table, i.e. the first of the six icons that appear there. You'll then be asked to select how many columns (vertical boxes) and rows (horizontal boxes) you'd like the table to include.

Above: You can simply insert a table into an existing content placeholder and selecting how many rows and columns you'd like to include.

If we use the bowling league analogy from above, we have five players and seven different headings for our information (names, games, points, strikes, etc.). That means we need a table with six columns and seven rows to fit everything in (see left).

Alternatively, if you select Insert from the Ribbon and then hit

Table (use Tables > New on a Mac), you can select a visual representation of the columns and rows you'll need. Hover over your preferred configuration with your mouse and click to insert the table into a pre-existing slide.

Drawing a Table

If you have a certain size in mind for your table, you can use the draw tool. On a PC, this is located in the Table drop-down arrow within Insert, while on a Mac it

Above: If you select Insert table from the Ribbon rather than from within the content placeholder you can choose from a visual representation of the columns and rows you'll need.

has a dedicated button in the Mac Tables tab. This tool will turn your cursor into a pencil and you can draw the shape as you would when drawing a content placeholder.

> ## Hot Tip
> Drawing a table seems like a roundabout way of doing things. Use the Insert Table tools and then just drag the corners to customize the size of the table within the slide.

In order to populate this blank shape with rows and columns, select Split Cells from the new Table Tools Layout tab and select the number of columns and rows you require.

Editing the Layout of Your Table

Once you've inserted your table, the layout is by no means set in stone. The Table Tools Layout tab, which appears in the Ribbon whenever you're working on a table, allows you to alter its size and that of individual cells easily, while adding/deleting new rows and columns. Here are the most important commands.

⊝ **Delete**: Hit this to shed a row or column from the table.

⊝ **Insert Above, Insert Below, Insert Left or Insert Right**: These add rows/columns depending on where the cursor currently sits within the table. If you've selected, for example, three rows, Insert Below will add three more rows beneath the cursor.

⊝ **Cell Size**: Select a cell to adjust the size of an entire row or column by using the up and down height and width boxes arrow (PC only).

⊝ **Distribute Rows and Distribute Columns**: These buttons will undo any height and width edits and return the cells to an even spread across the table.

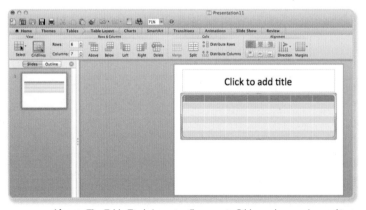

⊝ **Table Size**: To change table size, drag the corners of the table, but to more be precise, use the height/width arrows. Ticking the Lock Aspect Ratio box will ensure that everything stays within your pre-set proportions (PC only).

Above: The Table Tools Layout will appear in Ribbon when you're working on your table and allows you to alter its shape and size.

ADD STYLE

Once you're happy with the size, layout and content of your table, you can start adding a little panache. The default table style will always showcase colours that match your chosen theme, but you can change this with the Table Tools Design tab in the Ribbon, which appears when you're working on a table; here are some of the options.

Header Row/First Column: Highlights the top row in a darker shade. This can distinguish the information headings from the data.

Total Row/Last Column: If you're planning to add up scores in the bottom row or the last column then you can tick these boxes to draw attention to them.

Banded Columns/Rows: Ticking one of these boxes will apply alternate shades to each column or row – like a well-mown lawn.

Table Styles: As with pictures, videos and text, you can also add a little design panache to your table. Select the drop-down menu and choose from styles best matched to your theme, or from Light, Medium or Dark styles.

Shading (Fill on Mac): Select different shades from theme colours or standard colours. Keeping these relatively pale will make the information more visible.

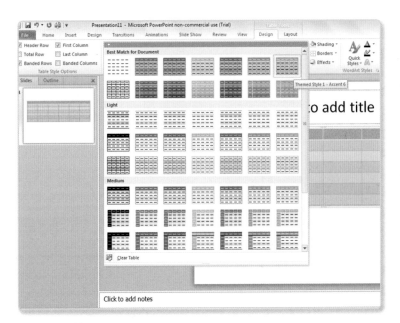

Borders: These add physical lines around selected cells. To make the individual cells stand out you should either colour band them (*see* screenshot to right) or use borders.

Above: Adding style to your table is very simple, just use the Design tools under the Table tools tab and start exploring your options.

→ **Effects**: Add a Bevel, Shadow or Reflection to the table. The latter is the neatest of these effects, whereas the Bevel effect feels a bit excessive.

OLDER VERSIONS?

In PowerPoint 2003, where there are no Ribbon tabs to speak of, you can select Tools > Object Options in order to customize the style and layout variables mentioned above.

Populating a New Table

You've erected your table – now comes the fun part: adding in all of the information. Just think of each box in the table as an independent text box. You can click within each one and the information you type will be totally self-contained to that box. When you're done, press Tab to move to the next box or click wherever you'd like to add more info. As you can see above, our bowling league table is now complete.

Above: To add information to your table, simply click each cell and type as you would in a normal text box.

Hot Tip

All text formatting tools are available to you when working within tables. These can be useful, for example, if you'd like to add bold emphasis to one or more pieces of information. You can also use the WordArt tools in the Table Tools Design tab.

CHARTS

Charts and graphs are the heartbeat of an information-heavy PowerPoint presentation. They're a fantastic, colourful and varied representation of data (sales figures, weather patterns, favourite ice cream flavours). Rather than simply looking at endless screens of numbers, charts can give an audience a visual perspective of your key points and arguments without making their eyes glaze over.

WHAT YOU'LL NEED

Before you start plotting your line graphs and bar graphs, you'll need a set of data: something to put along the x axis and something to put along the y axis.

TYPES OF CHART

Once you begin the process of adding a chart, you'll be asked to pick a type – here are the options.

- **Column:** Data is presented in vertical columns, while categories (days of the week, months, ice cream flavours, etc.) sit along the horizontal x axis.

- **Line:** These graphs plot data points across the horizontal X-axis. Data points are joined by a straight line.

- **Pie:** Perfect for showing proportional data, as the size of the slice will depend on the percentage of the data each category represents.

- **Bar:** A Column chart that somebody tipped on its side. Numbers will appear to stretch for the finish line rather than reach for the sky.

Area: These are used to emphasize trends over time, e.g. if the rainfall has tripled compared to last year.

X Y (Scatter): These graphs combine two sets of numeric data and mark the point where they would meet if a line was drawn from both axes. For example, if you'd like to see how rainfall relates to air temperature.

Stock: If market wheeling and dealing is your game, these charts can be used to plot the opening and closing numbers as well as the high and low points on any given day.

Surface: These charts take the appearance of a topographical map; a surface chart colour co-ordinates numbers within the same range. For example, 0–2 would be in blue, 2–4 would be in red and 4–6 would be in green.

Doughnut: A pie chart that someone ate the middle out of.

Bubble: These are similar to scatter charts, but the size of the bubble accounts for a third set of data: the x and y axes could plot temperature and rainfall data, whereas the size of the bubble would represent the wind speed.

Radar: Rather than using the X Y axis, a Radar chart anchors its data from a central point.

Right: The drop-down charts menu offers you a range of chart types.

Each of these chart types has many different incarnations. For example, a column chart can place the data side by side or stack the numbers into one column; you'll see the different styles underneath the relevant headings.

ADDING A CHART

Click the Insert Chart icon from within a content placeholder to summon a pop-up menu where you'll be asked to choose a chart type from those listed above (on Mac there's no pop-up; you just select from the Ribbon). Consider which is best for the data you plan to use, click it and hit OK. Alternatively, you can click within the placeholder, use the Insert tab and select Chart from the Illustrations pane.

These are the best options, as they make the best use of the space in the content placeholder. Adding a chart to a slide outside of a placeholder just pastes it over existing content – but don't worry, you can still move and resize to your exact specs using the methods we've become accustomed to.

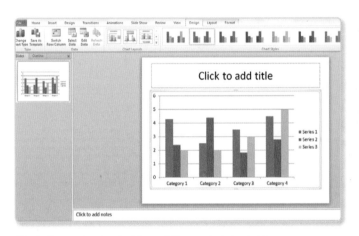

Above: You can insert a chart from within a content placeholder by clicking on the chart icon, this will summon a pop-up menu.

WORKING WITH EXCEL

When you choose a chart from the methods listed above, PowerPoint will call on the assistance of its partner, Excel. The number-crunching Microsoft Office stablemate will automatically launch and snap against PowerPoint so both programs appear together on the screen (not quite as fluid on a Mac; just adjust Window sizes to make it so).

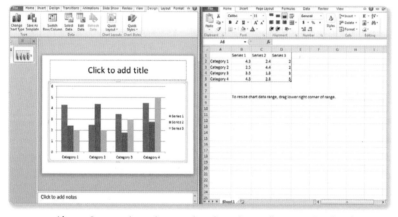

You'll see a default Excel document, called a datasheet, which supplies the information needed to populate the new chart you'll currently see on your screen. These placeholder numbers are just random series to give you a visual representation of how the chart will look.

Above: Once you have chosen a chart, PowerPoint will summon Excel so that you can enter your data.

OLDER VERSIONS? In PowerPoint 2003, adding a chart won't launch Excel but a built-in datasheet tool which can be customized in the same way.

Adding Your Own Data in Excel

Once the allied forces of PowerPoint and Excel are dominating your screen, we'll need to alter the data to our own. Editing these spreadsheets is the same as working within a PowerPoint table.

1. You'll initially see a list of four categories and three series of data. As the on-screen message says: 'To resize chart data range, drag lower right corner of range'. Dragging this blue marker in or out will add more, or delete, columns and rows to the chart.

2. We want enough room for seven days in the Category axis and three ice cream flavours in the Series value axis to chart our weekly sales.

3. Next, you need to change the names of your headings from Category 1, 2, etc. to the days of the week and then change the Series headings to add the names of the ice

cream flavours we're flogging. Just click in the relevant cell and overtype the existing data, and then add your numbers. We sold seven strawberry ice creams on Monday, so add that number where the two axes meet.

4. Updates to the numbers will immediately be reflected in a change to the chart within PowerPoint, which we think is thoroughly awesome.

Hot Tip

Excel also features a chart creation tool, so if you have an existing chart from that program that you'd like to copy to your PowerPoint slides, just copy and paste it (Select > Control+C to copy and then Control+P to paste in PowerPoint (PC) or select Command+C and Command+P (Mac)).

Changing Your PowerPoint Chart

If the chart you've selected doesn't quite offer the perfect visual representation of data you'd hoped for, it's easy to try a different option rather than deleting and starting from scratch.

Just select the chart and you'll see the new Chart Tools Design tab in the Ribbon. From this, select the Change Chart Type button and you'll be presented with the same options as if you were adding a chart from scratch – and all your data will remain intact.

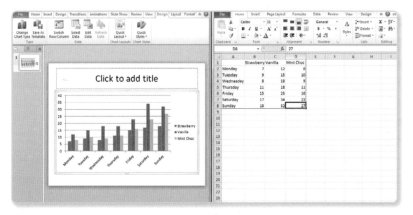

Above: If your chart does not look how you would like it to after the data has been entered, you can easily play around with chart types under the Change Chart Type button.

Tweaking the Design

The Chart Tools Design tab (PC only) features a host of tools that allow you to tweak the appearance of your table and further refine which data appears and how that data is presented. You'll see this tab emerge within the Ribbon when working with charts and, on the PC, the Chart Tools section contains three tabs: Design, Layout and Format. On the Mac, it's Charts, Chart Layout and Format.

Above: The Switch Row/Column button quickly applies the data to the opposite axis.

Switch Row/Column (Switch Plot on Mac)

This simple button lets you apply your data to the opposite axis. In our case, pressing this button means that the days of the week now appear in the y (vertical) axis, while the ice cream flavours reside within the x axis. Sometimes this can alter the visual perception of a chart; for instance, now the focus is more on the pattern of ice cream flavours rather than the sales each day.

Selecting, Editing and Refreshing Data

The three other buttons under the Data pane allow you to tweak which figures are translated from the Excel datasheet to the PowerPoint chart.

- ⊖ **Select Data:** Clicking this will summon a dialogue box from Excel (it's in the drop-down Edit button on a Mac). This can be used to tailor the range of data that appears within the chart. You can also add/edit labels to appear in the Legend.

Edit Data: Hitting this button just sends you back to Excel to make any changes to the datasheet.

Refresh Data: If you do end up changing the datasheet in Excel, the changes you make should automatically carry over to your chart. However, hitting this button will ensure your chart is updated with the most recent data (PC only).

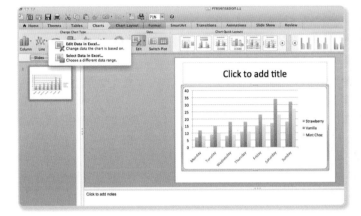

Above: The Select Data button (PC), or Edit Data button (Mac) within the Data pane allows you to control which figures are translated from the Excel datasheet to the chart in PowerPoint.

Changing the Layout

Finding the perfect chart for your presentation is a three-step process. Firstly, you pick the type of chart (Column, Bar, Pie, Scatter, etc.) and then you pick from the list of variables (clustered, stacked, 3-D, etc.); remember you will have taken the first two steps when adding your chart.

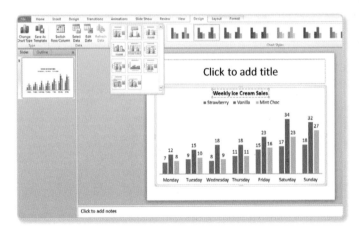

Above: After you have selected your chart style you can adjust the layout; simply choose from the options within the Chart Layout button in the Chart Tools Design tab.

The Chart Layouts button in the Chart Tools Design tab allows you to take the third step. As if those initial two choices weren't difficult enough, each chart type usually has around 10 different layouts to choose from. These are minor changes involving where the legend sits on the page,

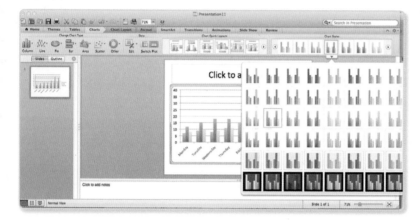

whether numbers are written on the columns and whether a data table also features on the chart.

Chart Styles

Wait! Just when you thought you were done, there's a fourth step. You can also select from the PowerPoint Styles

Above: There are also lots of pre-selected colour combinations for your chart to choose from!

drop-down menu featuring 48 (count 'em) different colour combinations for your chart. The row along the bottom places a black background behind your chart, which can sometimes make for easier reading.

CHART TOOLS LAYOUT TAB

The Chart Tools tabs in the Ribbon are massively confusing. Design features format options, Layout features format and design options, and Format features design and layout options. It's a big mess and we're not even going to begin to wonder why Microsoft put what where; we're just going to deal with each tool as we come to it.

Adding Titles, Legends, Labels and Data Tables

The Labels pane within the Layout tab is a really handy feature (Chart Layout on Mac). Here you can add a host of important data to make your chart clearer to the audience.

⊖   **Chart Title:** Use the drop-down menu to give your chart a name. In our case it's ' Weekly Ice Cream Sales'. Once you've selected the option, you can write it in on the slide.

Axis Titles: This can be handy in pinpointing what your x and y axes represent. Our x axis title is '6–11 August 2012' and our y axis is 'Most Popular Flavours'.

Legend: Most graphs come with a legend to illustrate which colours correspond to which data. However, this can be turned off or moved around using this button.

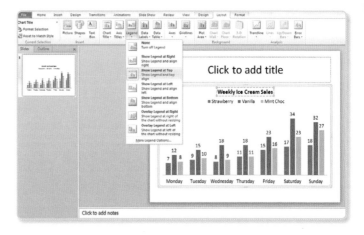

Above: The Labels pane is great for adding info that will make your chart clearer for your audience, such as titles and labels.

Data Labels: Most charts offer a visual representation of the comparisons without always reflecting exact numbers. Data labels can add these numbers into the chart and this tool allows you to position them accordingly.

Data Table: Most of the time we use charts so we don't have to make our audiences study boring oceans of numbers. However, if you want to supplement the chart with a data table underneath then be our guest.

PowerPoint Chart Analysis Tools

Here are a few tools to key your audience in on what's going on within your charts.

Error Bars: Within the Analysis pane you can add Error Bars, which could reflect the margin for potential error, as they do with political polls.

Up/Down Bars: If you're working with a line chart, for example, you can use these to add bars marking the gaps between the sets of data.

Lines: By selecting the Lines option, PowerPoint draws a line from the plotted point on the graph to the bottom of the x-Axis (almost a combination of a line and column chart).

Trendline: These can reflect an average or even offer projections based on your data. Adding a Trendline adds the data to your legend.

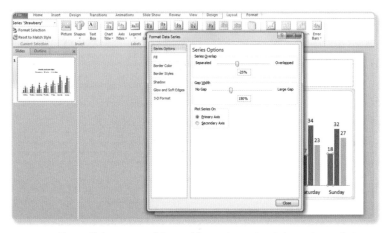

Above: If the amount of data and formatting options is becoming confusing, the Current Selection pane in the Charts Layout tab is really useful for working on individual parts of you chart

Formatting Each Element of Your Chart

Sometimes the level of detail in PowerPoint gets a little intimidating and this is one of those occasions. You can even format the Border Colours and Border Style.

In the Current Selection pane in the Layout tab you can use the drop-down menu to select an element of the table. We'll pick the Strawberry Ice Cream Sales series; from there you can hit the Format Selection button to make the adjustments mentioned above. If you think it's too much, hit the Reset to Match Style button (PC only).

Shape/Chart Styles

As with all of the other objects we've added to PowerPoint (pictures, videos, tables, etc.) there's a Format tab for adding final design touches and effects. The Shape Styles (PC) or Chart Styles (Mac) is the most useful tool here, as it can take a cluttered chart and give it a little panache. If you want to add a reflection to the chart like we did with a table, then use the Shape Effects button. Lastly, WordArt Styles are available to you for titles and legend items.

SMARTART

SmartArt is labelled as such because it's, well, pretty smart and quite arty. It aims to convert those endless slides of text-based information into visually appealing graphical designs featuring colourful shapes, logical progression points and sometimes photographs too. With well over 150 SmartArt styles on offer, we'll help you to achieve SmartArt nirvana.

TYPES OF SMARTART

Before we go about creating our SmartArt diagrams, let's introduce you to what's on offer and how the different categories can work for your presentation. Hit the Insert tab and then click the SmartArt button to bring up the options. You'll see the list of SmartArt categories listed on the left-hand side of the pop-up Window. Mac users have the advantage of a dedicated SmartArt tab within the PowerPoint ribbon.

- **List:** Livens up your bullet points and secondary points with neat design features, while some selections can also represent information that runs in a sequence.

- **Process:** Highlights a logical flow of information,

- **Cycle:** Shows a sequence of stages, ideas that that spring from a central theme or interrelated ideas.

- **Hierarchy:** Allows you to choose a key point of information and featuring the offshoots underneath. It could be great for a family tree or a chain of command.

- **Relationship:** Great for showcasing interlocking points like target lists, overlapping concepts like Venn diagrams or opposing ideas like pluses and minuses.

Matrix: These show related points in four quadrants.

Pyramid: Showcasing hierarchal relationships between the many and the few (accessed by the Other button on Mac).

Picture: A host of options that incorporate photos. For example, a photo of a tiger could lead into a list on numbers left in the wild.

Left: There are lots of SmartArt options to transform your data. Browse these choices by simply hitting the SmartArt button in the Insert tab.

Hot Tip

Each of these SmartArt categories has multiple styles within it. Hover over a thumbnail for a detailed explanation of where it could be useful and which elements of your text will be included (primary and secondary, or just primary). This will help you to decide which diagram is best for your information.

OLDER VERSIONS? PowerPoint 2003 does not feature a SmartArt tool. You can create diagrams yourself by using the very limited Diagram and Organisational Chart option in the Insert menu. However, you'll need to add text manually.

ADDING A SMARTART DIAGRAM

Although it's possible to add a SmartArt diagram and then populate it with pictures and text, we'd advise that you build the bullet-pointed or numbered lists before you start and then use the Convert to SmartArt tool.

As you've probably seen from examining the types of SmartArt available, the tool plays nicely with primary and secondary text information. Primary information is your key bullet points, while secondary information is the sub-points; these are usually represented by a dash and are indented beneath the bullet.

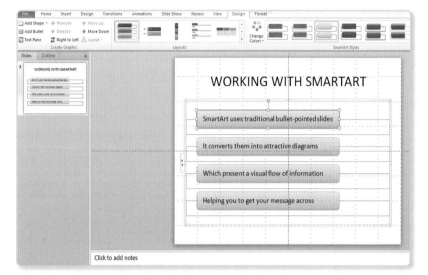

Above: Using the Convert to SmartArt tool is really simple as you can enter your information and then convert it to a SmartArt diagram.

Once you've selected the text (*see page 88*) you'd like to convert, right-click on it with your mouse and select Convert to SmartArt from the pop-up formatting box.

From here you'll be presented with some common options. Hover over them with your cursor and you'll instantly see a representation of how your information will look in that style. If you see one you like, click on it. To study the complete range of options listed on the previous page, hit More SmartArt Graphics until you find one you're happy with.

Hot Tip

If there are spelling mistakes in your text, right-clicking won't bring up the Convert to SmartArt option, so if you're not seeing it, make sure the text is highlighted and all of the spellings are correct – then try again.

Editing Text

You may have found the perfect 'Counterbalance arrows' design to represent the pluses and minuses of moving to a new city, but you still want to make some changes to the text. You can click the diagram itself and edit text within the slide, but that's a bit fiddly.

The Text Pane, which appears automatically when working with SmartArt, brings up a helpful Outline View style to look at your text. It can also be summoned from the arrows at the left edge of the shape, or by clicking Text Pane within the SmartArt Tools Design tab.

You can also add bullets, promote and demote paragraphs or move them up and down using the Create Graphic pane within the same tab. All of the tools appear automatically within the Text Pane for Mac users after you convert text to SmartArt.

Adding Finishing Touches

As with everything in PowerPoint, there's always something you can tweak and polish. The SmartArt tool is no different and allows you to add all of the neat design touches, effects and styles we've come to know and love with other PowerPoint objects. They are accessible from the Design Tools tab (PC) or Format tab (Mac) which pops up when working with SmartArt.

Above: The Design Tools tab lets you make all the usual tweaks and changes to your SmartArt.

As you can see, you can select alternate layouts, and change the colour scheme of the SmartArt (the default colours match your theme) and SmartArt Styles, if you'd like to get a little 3-D action going. The adjacent Format tab features all of the regular Shape Styles, WordArt Styles, Size and alignment tools. Also, all shapes added through SmartArt can be resized, rotated and relocated like any other objects within PowerPoint.

EQUATIONS

PowerPoint is well equipped to cope with the needs of scientists and mathematicians, who want to present their work via a slideshow, thanks to the Equation feature. This gives you a host of common equations to choose from and all of the symbols and formula structures required to build your own. Non-scientific minds can look away now.

ADDING EQUATIONS (PC ONLY)

Within the Insert tab of the Ribbon, you'll see a nice large Equation button. Hit the drop-down arrow to see a host of commonly used equations (Pythagorean Theorem, Binominal Theorum and more).

However, if you select Insert New Equation at the bottom of the menu or the Equation button itself, you'll be transported to a new tab: Equation Tools Design.

Within the content placeholder, you'll see highlighted text that says 'Type equation here'. Within this menu, you can insert your own symbols by clicking the appropriate one within the Symbols pane of the tab.

You can do the same with the various formula tools you'll see under the Structures pane. Each Fraction structure, Script structure, etc. has

Above: The Equation button is located within the Insert tab in Ribbon. From there you will find commonly used equations.

various options you can select from the drop-down menu. Once the structure is within your presentation, you'll see spaces for numbers and letters represented by small boxes with dotted lines. Click within these to overwrite with your own data.

Equations on Mac

Again, things are slightly different on Macs as the built-in Equation tool isn't present. In order to insert an equation into your presentation, the easiest way is to use the functionality in Microsoft Word (where it *is* present) and copy it into your PowerPoint presentation.

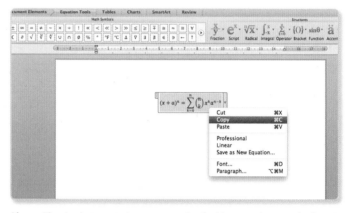

Above: The simplest way to insert an equation for Mac users is to use the Equation tool in word and simply copy and paste it into your PowerPoint presentation.

Hot Tip

When typing an equation, PowerPoint attempts to use regular keyboard strokes and convert them to how they may be used in equations. Let it do its work. When you press Enter to complete your equation, PowerPoint will automatically format the equation.

1. Open a new Microsoft Word document.

2. Click the Insert Menu and scroll down to Equation.

3. You'll now see the Equation Tools tab within the Ribbon and a self-contained box within your document that says 'Type equation here'.

4. Use the Symbols and Structures tools as explained on the previous page.

5. When your equation is complete, select the text, and copy and paste into your PowerPoint placeholder.

DRAWING SHAPES AND OBJECTS

While SmartArt offers a huge array of pre-set, fabulously designed graphics to spice up your information, if you fancy yourself as a bit of an artist, there's also a host of pre-set drawing tools you can use to annotate your slides. You can use shapes as design tools to connect information.

DRAWING SIMPLE SHAPES

In order to add shapes to your slides, click the Insert tab and select the Shapes button in the Illustrations pane (PC) or hit Home > Shapes on a Mac to obtain a drop-down menu of options. Once you've selected your shape, you can point your cursor back to your slide. As soon as you hold down the left button and begin moving the mouse, you'll start drawing.

Drag the cursor out and the shape will be created before your eyes. When it reaches the size and proportions (height to width) of

Hot Tip

If you want your shape to appear on every slide within your presentation, draw it on the Master Slide. For Master Slide tips head to page 129.

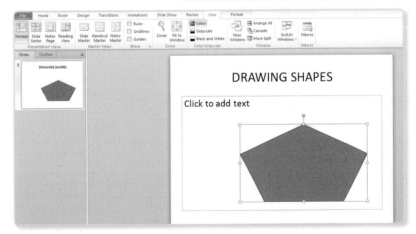

Above: Select the Shapes button under the Insert tab (PC), or the Home tab for Mac users. Then simply hold down the left mouse button and start drawing.

your choice, you can take your finger off the mouse button. The shape will be fitted with a colour to match your theme but, of course, this can be changed.

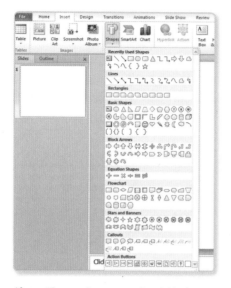

Above: There is a huge range of available shapes, just browse through the drop-down menu.

Types of Shapes

Selecting the drop-down Shapes button presents you with a staggering array of available shapes (Mac users can access shape styles through Home Shapes > Shape Browser).

Here are the options:

⊖ **Recently Used Shapes:** Here you'll see the shapes you've recently used.

⊖ **Lines:** A great way to link information within your slides. There's also a host of arrow connectors, straight and curved lines. When drawing curved lines, you'll need to click at the point where you'd like the line to curve and continue drawing.

⊖ **Rectangles:** Most commonly used for adding text. You can also draw shapes with one or more corners cut off, for a more unique feel.

⊖ **Basic Shapes:** Here you can add a host of commonly used shapes, such as circles and triangles, but also objects like smiley faces, weather symbols, 3-D cubes and more.

Hot Tip

Once you've drawn your shape, use the Control handle (yellow indicator) to customize the proportions. For example, if you've drawn a star, move the control handle in and out to determine the size and depth of its points.

Block Arrows: Helping you to connect information with four-way arrows, arced arrows and more.

Equation Shapes: Add a plus, minus, divide by, multiply and equal sign, among others.

Flowchart: SmartArt does a decent job of creating flowchart-like objects, but you can design your own with this series of shapes and some help from some of the above (lines, arrows, equations, etc.).

Stars and Banners: Useful shapes.

Callouts: Customizable speech bubbles which you can easily add text to.

> **OLDER VERSIONS?**
> In PowerPoint 2003 you can use the AutoShapes button within the lower toolbar.

Action Buttons: For use with clickable slides (*see* page 193. You can draw a play button, add a link and an action to it, and your media clip will then play.

Customizing Your Shapes

As we discussed when creating a text box (*see* page 128), you can resize, move and rotate a shape using the on-screen tools. Dragging the Sizing handle (white bubble) allows you to control the size, while clicking anywhere within the shape lets you drag it to a new position. Clicking the Rotation handle

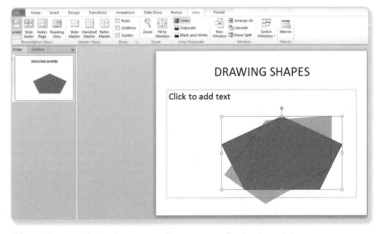

Above: Once you have chosen your shape you can alter its size, rotation and position as much as you like using the on-screen tools.

(green bubble) will allow you to drag-to-rotate, but you can also use the Rotate button in the Drawing Tools tab to rotate in multiples of 90 degrees.

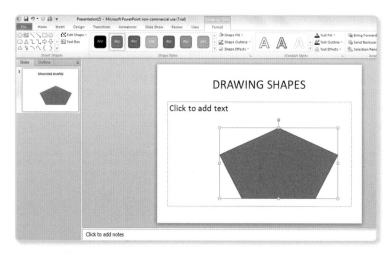

Above: There are plenty of options for changing the colour, effect and outline of your shape using the Drawing Tools Format tab.

Adding Style to Your Shapes

In order to avoid repeating ourselves multiple times, we won't go into too much detail here, but within the Drawing Tools Format Tab, you can choose from the drop-down menus of Shape Styles, Shape Effects (e.g. Bevel, Shadow, Reflection and 3-D), Shape Fill and Shape Outline.

Drawing Freehand

Within the Insert Shapes menu, you can select the Freeform tool from the Lines section (PC) or Lines and Connectors (Mac). This will turn your cursor into a pen tool and allow you to start drawing on your slide.

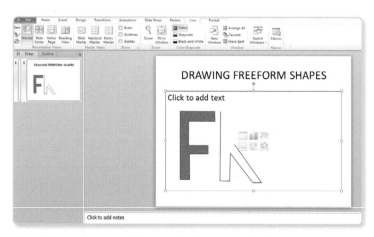

Above: The combinations of shapes and styles are almost limitless!

Hot Tip

If you're unhappy with your shape but have spent forever adding text, colour and effects, there's no fun in deleting it and starting again. Just click Edit Shape to change the shape style without losing the formatting.

Click the cursor where you'd like to begin drawing, hold it down and then move your mouse or trackpad. When you're done drawing, double-click, otherwise the pen tool will assume you want to carry on. If you'd like to complete a shape, double-click at the point where you started drawing.

Drawing Freeform Shapes

The Freeform Line tool comes in really handy when creating your own shapes. After selecting the tool (Insert > Shapes > Lines > Freeform), click once at your start point, then release the mouse and move to draw a straight line. Click again when you'd like to form a corner and continue. If you'd like to go completely freehand at any point during this process, just hold down the mouse button. Again, when you've finished drawing the shape, return to your start point and click.

Hot Tip

When drawing freehand, summon the slide gridlines for a handy visual indicator. In order to access this, hit the View tab (PC) or View > Guides (Mac) and tick the Guidelines box.

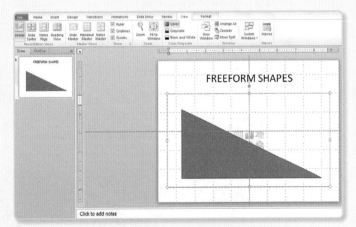

Above: The gridlines come in handy when drawing shapes freehand.

ADVANCED POWERPOINT

HYPERLINKS & CLICKABLE SLIDES

Hyperlinks allow you to insert a clickable link from one object on a PowerPoint slide which, when clicked, will summon another slide within your presentation. They can also be used to bring up a completely different presentation from within PowerPoint or a document from other Microsoft Office programs like Word or Excel. You can use a hyperlink to bring up something from your computer (music from iTunes or Spotify, or a photo from one of your albums). You can also utilize hyperlinks to load pages from the internet and you'll also be able to click to send an email right from the slide.

CREATING A HYPERLINK

Choose the object from which you'd like to link. It can be anything within PowerPoint: a placeholder, a shape, a word or a line of text, a video, photo, chart or table. Once you've selected it with the mouse button, hit Insert from the Ribbon and choose Hyperlink (on Mac, choose Insert > Text > Hyperlink from the Home tab).

When you click Hyperlink (or hit the Control/Command+K shortcut), you'll be presented with a pop-up dialogue box, from which you have to select the item you'd like to link to (see left).

Left: Once you have chosen to add the Hyperlink through the Insert tab you must choose the item to link it to in the pop-up dialogue box.

Hyperlink to a Computer File

To bring up an existing presentation or another document on your PC/Mac, hit Insert > Hyperlink and stick with the pre-selected 'Existing File or Web Page' tab from the pop-up window. You'll see the Current Folder, but you can navigate beyond this by using the arrow or the other tools next to drop-down menu marked My Documents. Check the Recent Files tab if you know you've been working within that document in the not too distant past. It may be there waiting for you. Once you've found the file or program of your choice, press OK.

Hyperlink to a Slide Within the Presentation

This is a fine option if you'd like to create a Contents slide for your presentation or if you'd like to jump from one section to another within a long presentation.

From the Insert Hyperlink window select the 'Place in This Document' tab which brings up a list of all of the slides within your presentation. Clicking a slide will bring up a preview and if this is the one you'd like to link to then press OK. Mac users can make use of Anchors within the Hyperlink options. Anchors can be used to link to a place within the current document. Hit Select File to choose the desired presentation, then press Locate within the Anchor section.

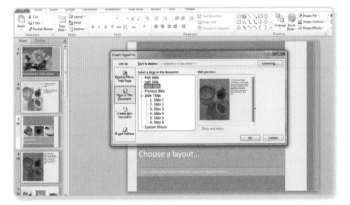

Above: You can use Hyperlinks within your presentation to jump between pages non-chronologically, for example if using a contents page.

Hot Tip

To create a Contents slide, add a new Title and Placeholder slide immediately following your first title slide. Use the content placeholder to write a numbered list of sections or slide titles and then use the Hyperlink tool to add the link to each section.

Above: You can add a Hyperlink to a webpage by pasting the URL link into the Address box of the Insert Hyperlink pop-up window.

Hyperlink to a Web Page

If you'd like to call on information from a page on the internet – offering further reading for your audience, a link to a video or a photo gallery – you can launch a web page from your PowerPoint presentation.

In order to achieve this, select your object as normal and bring up the Insert Hyperlink Window by selecting Insert > Hyperlink (Home > Insert Text > Hyperlink on a Mac). Using the Existing File or Web Page tab you can simply paste the relevant internet link (e.g. www.office.com) into the Address box and click OK. Alternatively, it may appear in the Browsed Pages tab.

Hyperlinking to a New Document or Email Address

You can link an object within PowerPoint to the opening of a brand new PowerPoint Document. Click the 'Create New Document' tab from the Edit Hyperlink Window. You can choose a name and folder destination for your presentation, and whether to start editing now or later.

You can also hyperlink to an email address of your choice, meaning that when this link is clicked, it will open a blank email address in the user's email client (Outlook for PC, Mail for Mac). This is great if people in your audience are navigating through the presentation by themselves and you want to encourage further contact or feedback.

Hot Tip

You can only click Hyperlinks while working within the Slide Show view, so you may like to preview the presentation to test all of your links work. Only text changes its appearance when you add hyperlinks (adding a blue underline), while all other objects remain the same.

USING ACTION BUTTONS

You may recall that when we covered adding shapes to your presentation (*see* page 83) we introduced items called Action Buttons. These shapes such as, forward, back, beginning, end, home, information and more, are perfect for anchoring information within your PowerPoint presentation.

They can be used to move forwards and backwards within the presentation, play a media clip or jump to the end of the presentation. They, like hyperlinked objects, can be used to launch web pages or new documents. As with Hyperlinks, Action Buttons only work when you're delivering the presentation .

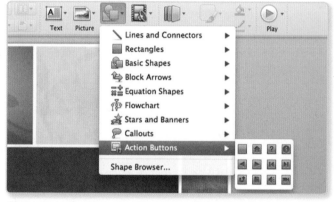

Above: Action buttons are an attractive way of controlling your slideshow. They carry commands so you can use them as links to other pages, etc, throughout your presentation.

Types of Action Buttons

Once you've added an Action Button, there's not always a lot of customizing you need to do, as most come loaded with actions befitting the icon. There are 12 Action Buttons to choose from and you can, of course, customize them how you wish, should you like to add a different action.

- **Back**: By default, adding this arrow will allow you to move back one slide.

- **Forward**: The default action takes you forward one slide.

- **End**: Clicking this button will take you to the end of the presentation.

- **Start**: Return to the beginning of a presentation.

Home: Another button to take you back to the beginning.

Information: No default action, so you'll need to apply one (see below). This would be ideal for linking to an external source, such as a website or datasheet containing more info.

Return: The default action takes you to the last viewed slide.

Movie: No default action applied, but would be useful for linking to a video on your computer or on the internet.

Document: No default action for this button, but logic suggests you'd want to use this to launch a Word document.

Sound: Want to play a piece of music from within your presentation, on your computer or from the internet? Hyperlink it to this button.

Help: No default action for the button, but if your presentation was running in an exhibit, a help button could be used to direct visitors to further information on the internet

Blank: No default action here either. Do with this as you may, or even draw your own action.

Adding Action Buttons to Your Slides

1. In order to add one of these buttons, identify the slide and click the Insert tab in the Ribbon. From the drop-down Shapes menu, you'll see Action Buttons; click on the icon that best suits your intended action.

Hot Tip

Actions can be added to any object within PowerPoint, not just the custom Action Buttons within Shapes. To add an action to a picture, text box or chart, select it and hit Insert > Action and then follow the instructions below.

2.   Draw it on your slide as you normally would by holding down the mouse button and dragging it to the size you want.

3.   This will automatically summon the Action Settings Window, but you can also bring this up by selecting Action from the Insert tab (right click the button and select Action Settings on Mac). If you're happy with the default action, just press OK, but here's where you can customize Action Buttons to your own ends

4.   Action Buttons can be called into service by clicking on them or simply by hovering the mouse over them. You'll see the two options represented by separate tabs in the Action Settings Window. Here you can move between the two tabs (Mouse Click and Mouse Over) and then select your Action (*see* right).

Types of Action

Action Buttons work much like Hyperlinks. You can use the Action Settings menu to link to anywhere in your presentation, another PowerPoint presentation, another file on your computer or an internet URL. However, there are a few more options here: you can run a program like Office, Excel or iTunes, or run a Macro (a custom-built mini-program – a bit advanced for our needs, but for further reading go to Office.com/help and type in Macros). Last but not least, you can also use them to play a sound, as we did with slide transitions (*see* page 118).

Above: Select the action that you want your button to have by clicking on, or hovering your mouse over, it.

Hot Tip

As with Hyperlinks, you can use the Master Slide editor to add multiple Action Buttons which appear on all of your slides.

COLLABORATING ON PRESENTATIONS

Quite often, when producing PowerPoint presentations, the responsibility of creating and delivering the slide show won't always fall on your own shoulders; work colleagues, family members or classmates are also involved. Thankfully, the software comes equipped with tools for group sharing, modification and commenting.

SHARING YOUR PRESENTATION

If you're working as a team and have taken control of the presentation, it's likely that the rest of the group are going to want to have an input on the content – and besides, it's good to have feedback from your peers. PowerPoint has plenty of sharing tools that can get your work to colleagues, quickly and easily.

Sharing Your Presentation on a Mac

As we've already seen, PowerPoint for Mac doesn't use a Backstage View (as the PC version does). The tools we're about to discuss are mostly all there but are dotted around the program.

- The Share Using Email Attachment and Permissions buttons live within the Review tab in the Ribbon.

- To access SharePoint or SkyDrive or send to iPhoto, click File on the top menu then Share. On the File menu you also have the Reduce File Size options.

Before You Share

Before we start distributing our presentation to the world, there are a few housekeeping matters to take care of. Hit the File tab to access the Backstage View and you'll see the Info pane highlighted in orange. These options will help you to manage the file size for easier sharing, to protect your slide show from unwanted edits and to ensure that it is compatible for other users. Here are the key checks you should make.

Above: The Backstage View helps you to manage things like file size, permissions and performance options, so ensure you make the relevant checks before sharing your presentation.

- **Media Size and Performance:** If your presentation contains lots of video or audio content, then the file could be reaching a size where sharing is difficult and, in the case of email, impossible. This tab will inform you of the size of media files and give you the chance to change the quality from Presentation Quality to Internet Quality or Low Quality for easier sharing.

- **Permissions:** If you don't want others to change the presentation you can select Mark as Fina' to prevent edits or you can take the extra step of applying a password to ensure only those with the password can open the file.

- **Prepare For Sharing:** This drop-down menu will help to inspect for and get rid of cropped picture content, comments and annotations, and presentation notes. It'll also make sure that the presentation is readable by those with disabilities and it will point out any errors.

SENDING YOUR PRESENTATION VIA EMAIL

Once you've performed all the checks explained on the previous page and are happy with your PowerPoint presentation, the simplest way to send it is through the built-in Share Using Email functionality. To achieve this, make sure the newest version of the Presentation is saved (Control/Command+S).

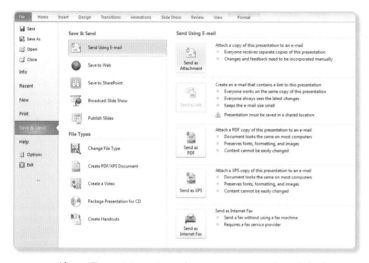

Above: The easiest way to send your presentation is through the Save and Send option within PowerPoint

Enter the Backstage View through the File tab and select the Save & Send option. Here you can select Send Using Email and then Send as Attachment. This will load the presentation up in your email client (Outlook on PC; instructions for accessing this feature on Mac can be found on page 196). Add the email addresses into the new email and hit Send.

You can also use the Send Using Email tab to send a link to the presentation, if it's already saved in a shared location (see opposite). This is great for larger presentations with too large file sizes to share as email attachments or if you'd like everyone working from the same document.

Hot Tip

Using the Save and Send option means everyone gets a copy of the presentation; therefore any changes and feedback made to it will need to be added manually to the master document. This can be great if you want to vet any changes.

Sending as PDF or XPS document (see file types on page 40) will allow the document to be viewed on computers that don't have PowerPoint and will preserve all of your text formats and images. If you select this option, PowerPoint will automatically convert the document and load it as an email attachment. In the absence of the Backstage View for Mac, these options are displayed within the File menu in PowerPoint.

In desperate times you can send by an Internet Fax, from the Save & Send menu within the Backstage View.

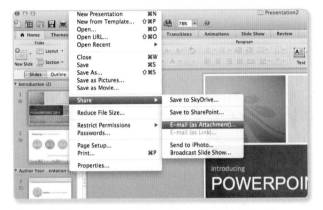

Above: The Share settings for Macs are located within the top File menu.

SAVING YOUR PRESENTATION ONLINE

> ## Hot Tip
>
> **Use the Change File Type option within the Save & Send section of the Backstage View and choose Save As > PowerPoint 97–2003 Presentation. This will ensure that those running older versions of PowerPoint – perhaps on old work or school PCs – will be able to open the presentation.**

In Chapter one (see page 41) we covered saving a PowerPoint file to Microsoft's SkyDrive online storage platform, but it's also possible to save online using the business-centric SharePoint Collaboration tool.

Sharing via SkyDrive is a solution everyone can use. In order to share this way, you'll need a Microsoft-hosted email address (Windows Live, Hotmail, Outlook.com, etc.) with which you get

25GB free SkyDrive Storage. You'll be asked to enter the login details for this account when selecting the Save to Web option but after that saving is simple and you'll see the presentation upload to SkyDrive.

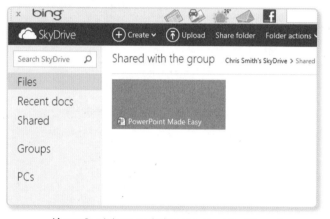

Above: Simply log in to skydrive.com or use the Microsoft SkyDrive link to access your presentation once it has been uploaded.

Working Within SkyDrive

Once the document is uploaded to SkyDrive, you can access it by using the Microsoft SkyDrive link in the Save to Web pane (see screenshot left) or by going to skydrive.com and logging in. Once there you'll see the presentation listed in your documents.

Now you're able to control who has access to the file or folder and the permissions they have. Click the Share option in the horizontal menu within the SkyDrive Window and then add email addresses and people from your contacts book to send them a link to the document (see screenshot to left).

You can also create View only, View and edit and Public links to the document by using the Get a link tab. Copy those links and share them with your group through whatever means you'd like. All of these share options can be amended whenever you like.

Above: Use the Share facility in SkyDrive to send chosen others a link to your document.

Recipients of the presentation don't need a SkyDrive account (through Hotmail, Live.com, Outlook.com) or PowerPoint installed to view the shared presentation; it will simply open in the web browser (Internet Explorer, Firefox, Chrome, etc.).

OLDER VERSIONS? SkyDrive wasn't invented when PowerPoint 2003 and 2007 arrived. They probably hadn't heard of cloud computing then, hence no SkyDrive pre-PowerPoint 2010.

Above: Recipients of the presentation can simply open your presentation in a web browser, without the need for PowerPoint or SkyDrive.

Hot Tip

If you're planning to share your presentation with the world you can use the 'Post to' tab within SkyDrive to post a link on Twitter. This will allow anyone to access it.

Above: You can share your presentation on Twitter by using the Post to tab within SkyDrive.

Editing using SkyDrive

The web-editing tools on PowerPoint are fantastic. Your recipients don't even need PowerPoint installed on their PC to edit the presentation; it can all be done using the Office web apps available on SkyDrive using the Edit in Browser tool.

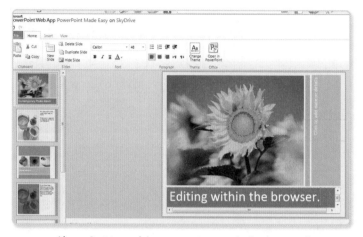

Above: Recipients of the presentation can edit the document by using the Office web apps available on SkyDrive.

The PowerPoint web app is a scaled back version of the desktop app. It allows users to amend text and pictures themes, and to insert pictures, SmartArt, Clip Art and links. All changes will be automatically saved back to the document on SkyDrive. Everyone with whom you've shared the document will see the same version, but only one person at a time will be able to work on the slide show.

Once everyone is happy with the changes, you can select the 'Open in PowerPoint' button and then Compare the presentation (see page 203) in order to accept or reject the changes made by the group.

Share to a SharePoint Location

This business-centric tool from Microsoft allows people to author presentations and to work on them at the same time. SharePoint is usually a tool used by businesses to improve employee productivity and to allow them to collaborate and work together even when out of the office.

If your place of work, school or college uses SharePoint, you can select this tool from the Backstage View to save the file to a shared location (File > Save & Send > Save to SharePoint > Browse for Location > Save As), where colleagues will be able to access from a shared online location and even work on the same presentation at the same time. If you're interested in acquiring SharePoint for your business, then head to sharepoint.microsoft.com for more information.

COMMENTING & COMPARING

As we mentioned in the sharing section, if someone in your work group has added changes through a different version of the document, you can either accept all of these and present the amended version or vet them by comparing them with the original.

USING THE COMPARISON TOOLS

If other people in your group have made changes to the presentation, it's easy to check these against the original:

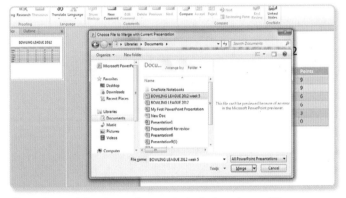

Above: Picture 1: By selecting Compare in the Review tab you will be requested to Merge the new and edited document.

1. Open the unedited version of the presentation and hit Compare in the Review tab, where you'll be requested to Merge the new and edited document (make sure it's saved on your computer; *see* Picture 1).

2. Rather than opening the new document alongside the unedited presentation, PowerPoint will bring up an action pane containing all of

Hot Tip

No changes will be made to your document until you accept them, which means viewing them and making a judgement is difficult. To view the amended version of the slide and Accept or Reject the changes based on that, double-click the slide within the Revisions tab.

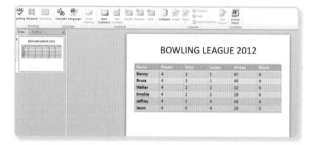

Above: Picture 2: PowerPoint will provide you with an action pane containing all the amendments made to each particular slide.

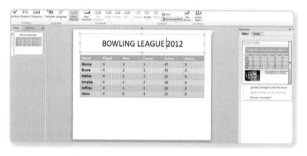

Above: Picture 3: Once you have compared changes, you can choose to accept or reject them.

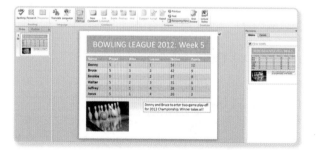

Above: Picture 4: No changes will be made to your document until you accept them. Once you have done this they will appear in the normal PowerPoint window.

the amendments made to each particular slide, while a Revisions tab will also appear on the left of the Window (*see* Picture 2).

3. You can use the Compare pane within the Review tab to 'Accept' or 'Reject' these changes on an individual level using the buttons within. The drop-down arrows within the Compare pane will allow you to accept or reject all changes on a slide or within an entire presentation.

4. In this instance, we're updating the standings in our bowling league table, which we created in the last chapter. A member of the final team has added the latest results and spruced up the design, with shape fills, a shadow effect on the table and a piece of Clip Art alongside some new information. We can choose to accept or reject the changes made to the slide (*see* Picture 3).

5. Once you're happy you've dealt with all the changes and either accepted or rejected them (*see* Picture 4), hit End Review in the Compare section to return to the normal PowerPoint Window.

OLDER VERSIONS? The Compare and Merge tool exists in PowerPoint 2003 (accessible from the Reviewing toolbar), but the feature was ditched in 2007. It's back by popular demand in PowerPoint 2010.

USING COMMENTS

Adding Post-it Notes-like comments to slides within PowerPoint can provide great reminders for changes you need to make or, if someone is reviewing the presentation, it can be a great way for them to make suggestions without messing with your beautifully designed slides.

Adding Comments to Slides

1. In order to add a comment, simply select the item within a slide that you'd like to comment on and hit the New Comment button (New on Mac) on the Review tab.

2. This will bring up the sticky note where you can begin to type and add your suggestions (e.g. 'I think we need a different picture here' or 'You've spelt contemporary incorrectly'.)

Above: You can add comments to your document for others to see when addressing editing issues.

3. All comments will be identified within the presentation by a small indicator with the initials of the person who wrote them and the comment number (for example, CS1). Clicking this will bring up the comment note.

4. You can edit the comments, delete them or move between them using the previous and next buttons on the Review tab. You can show or hide comments using the Show Markup button (Show on Mac).

TRANSPORTING YOUR PRESENTATION

If you're planning to deliver the presentation from your own computer then you won't need this section. However, if you're on the move and need to transport your entire presentation elsewhere you could always email it to yourself and share it to SkyDrive or SharePoint. There are other options, though, if you want a plan B or don't have access to the internet at your new destination.

BURN TO A CD OR DVD

This is a great option for transporting your presentation if it's too large to email or upload to SkyDrive/SharePoint. In the Backstage View (File tab in the Ribbon on PC) hit the Package Presentation for CD option (PC only).

Above: A good way of transporting your presentation is by burning it onto a CD or DVD.

Here you can select which slide shows you'd like to include within your presentation by using the Add/Remove buttons. Insert a blank CD into your disc drive and press Copy to CD. The wonders of modern technology will do the rest. All you need to do then is to insert the new CD into a PowerPoint-equipped machine and you'll be able to present on that computer.

OLDER VERSIONS? PowerPoint 2003 features a 'Package for CD' option in the File menu, whereas PowerPoint 2007 users can press the Office button and select Publish and Package for CD.

EXTERNAL HARD DRIVE OR MEMORY STICK

The tech world is moving beyond CDs and DVDs as storage media; they're too easily damaged and often don't offer enough space for our needs. You may like to save your presentation to a memory stick (often called pen drives or flash drives, *see* image above) or a fully-fledged external hard drive. Both of these will usually plug into the USB ports of your computer.

In order to move the file to the new drive, first plug it into your computer and then open the file viewer. Now find the PowerPoint presentation(s) you'd like to take with you, copy it and then paste it within the hard drive's window (you can also just drag and drop it).

BROADCASTING AND VIDEOING

You don't have to be standing in front of your audience in order to deliver your PowerPoint presentation – in most cases you'd probably rather not be.

LET THE WHOLE WORLD SEE!

PowerPoint 2010 (PC) and PowerPoint 2011 (Mac) have a feature enabling users to broadcast their presentation live to the entire world or record a video of it which can then be uploaded to the internet to be viewed any time.

Both can come complete with a narrated audio track recorded by you and pre-set timings for slide progression. It's much easier than you think it would be but, before we start, there are a few things we need to do to prepare our presentation.

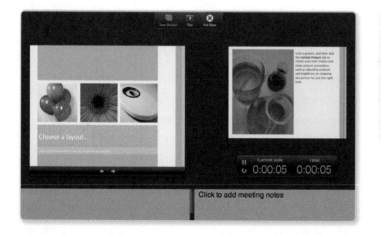

OLDER VERSIONS?
Unfortunately, PowerPoint 2003 doesn't have the facility to broadcast presentations or turn them into video.

Left: You can add narration and other audio to go alongside your slides.

CREATING A NARRATION TRACK

Before you broadcast to millions or create a video to upload on YouTube, you may want to record an audio track, as you're not going to be present to talk through the information on each of your slides:

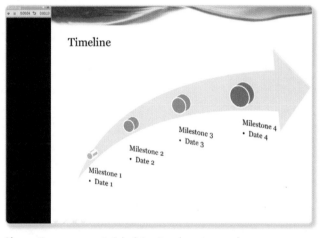

Above: Use your computer's built in microphone to record your narration, and keep track of the time by looking at the Recording box in the top left-hand corner.

1. From the Slide Show menu select Record Slide Show and make sure the 'Narrations and laser pointer' box is ticked. PowerPoint will enter full-screen Slide Show mode and the recording timer will start. You'll see it in the top left of the screen.

2. Speak into the built-in microphone on your computer and your narrations will be recorded. When you've progressed through the slide show and it comes to an end, the presentation will be recorded along with the narrations.

3. To ensure that they play during a broadcast or video recording, make sure the Play Narrations box is ticked within the Set Up pane of the Slide Show tab.

Hot Tip

The internal microphone on most computers is horrible. If you would like your audience to decipher your words our advice would be to invest in a USB microphone. They're usually plug-and-play, which means you can insert them into your USB port and they'll take over as the default mic on your PC.

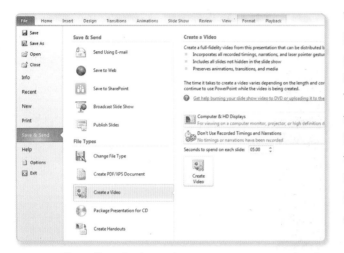

Above: If you decide to make your presentation into a video, you need to choose how many seconds you want to spend on each slide.

When to Avoid Timings

If you'd rather control the presentation by hand during the broadcast, you can deselect Use Timings. For a video you'll need timings, as you'll be unable to control it yourself. Therefore, when creating the video (*see* screenshot to left), PowerPoint will ask you to choose how long you want it to dwell on each slide (this is set at 5 seconds).

USING THE LASER POINTER

As you're not going to be physically present to point to the most important information, you can use PowerPoint's built-in laser pointer functionality when recording a slide show (PC only).

↪ To add a laser pointer to your broadcast or video, click Record Slide Show and make sure that the Narrations and laser pointer box is ticked, and then start to record.

Hot Tip

When recording your slide show to broadcast or for video, don't talk while moving between slides. Finish your sentence and pause. This will prevent you being cut off in mid-sentence when you progress through the presentation.

↪ To bring up the laser pointer, press and hold down Control and the left mouse button on your PC, and then move the mouse or trackpad around. When you have finished recording the slide show, the laser will be included in the broadcast or video.

BROADCASTING YOUR PRESENTATION

OK – now we're ready to go live! This is one of the cleverest tricks in the book (both this book and PowerPoint's!). Your presentation can be broadcast live to anyone with an internet connection and a computer; they don't even need to use PowerPoint, as it's totally web-browser based. All that's needed is for you to log into your Microsoft-based email account (Windows Live, Hotmail, etc.) to start the broadcast. Just like a conference call, a link will simply be sent to recipients who you want to tune in.

Starting a Web Broadcast

Here's what you need to do in order to begin broadcasting a presentation:

1. Select the option Save & Send in the Backstage View (for Mac users, it's File > Share > Broadcast Slide Show): see Picture 1.

2. If you haven't already logged in using your Windows Live ID (Hotmail, Outlook.com, etc.), you'll be asked to do so and, once that is complete, hit Start Broadcast.

3. It'll take about a minute to connect to the Broadcast Service (depending on your internet speed and the size of the presentation). Once that's done, you'll be gifted with a web link to send to your

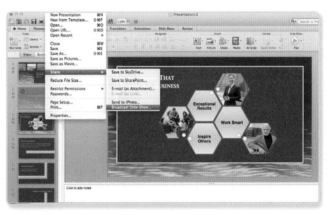

Above: Picture 1: You can choose to start a broadcast from the Save & Send option in the Backstage View (or from File > Share for Mac users).

Above: Picture 2: Once PowerPoint has connected to the Broadcast Service you will be given a web link to send to your recipients.

intended recipients (*see* Picture 2 on previous page). You can send it in an email or copy the link to do with as you wish.

4. Recipients of the link will be taken to a holding screen on their web browser, emblazoned with the placeholder: 'Waiting for Broadcast to begin' (*see* Picture 3).

5. Once you're happy that all of your viewers are tuning in (give it a couple of minutes!), hit Start Slide Show and you're away.

Above: Picture 3: Your recipients will see a holding screen until you are ready to broadcast.

Delivering the Broadcast

If you've added timings, narrations and a laser-pointer guide to your presentation then you don't have to do anything once you've hit Start Slide Show. The presentation will run simultaneously on your screen and that of the viewers. When the presentation is complete, the broadcast will end.

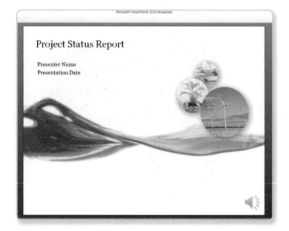

If you're going to control the slides by hand, you can use all of the tools normally available to you (*see* page 81). As you click Next Slide, Previous Slide, Play a media item, and so on, the change will be reflected on your viewers' screens within fractions of a second. All animations, transitions and effects will also be visible to your audience. Pretty cool, huh?

left: As you control the presentation, your recipients will experience what is happening on your screen.

MAKE A VIDEO

The second way to ensure your presentation reaches your audience without you being physically in the room is by creating a video of your presentation. This video can be shared on DVD, memory stick, or it can be placed on an online storage portal (like SkyDrive) or uploaded to a video sharing site like YouTube. A video version of the presentation is also a great backup to have if you know you'll be presenting somewhere without PowerPoint or the internet. There are few nuances between the PC and Mac versions of PowerPoint; here's how to create a video for both.

How to Create a Video on PC

1.   Hit File to enter the Backstage View and, within the Save & Send pane, select the option Create a Video (*see* Picture 1).

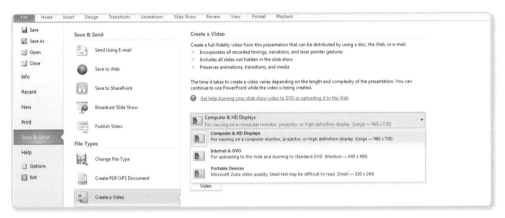

Above: Picture 1: Create a video from the Save & Send pane within the Backstage View tab.

2.   Within this screen you'll see two drop-down menus in the centre and the first controls video quality.

⟳   **Large:** The highest resolution (960 x 720 in 4:3 aspect ratio), suitable for viewing on computers and HD TVs, but it will take longer to upload to the internet due to a larger file size.

Medium: Good quality (640 x 480 resolution); ideal for uploading online or burning to a DVD.

Small: The Portable Devices setting brings the lowest quality on offer (320 x 240). File size will be lower, but text may be difficult to read.

3.   The second drop-down menu relates to the slide timings and narrations you have recorded for your video.

Use Recorded Timings and Narrations: The default setting. It wants to include your audio track and the slide progression schedule you learned to employ in this section. If you recorded the slide show using a laser pointer, this will also be included.

Don't Use Recorded Timings and Narrations: Select this to create the video without a voice track and to rely on a pre-set duration for each slide, which can be controlled using the 'Seconds to spend on each slide' panel below this menu (see Picture 2).

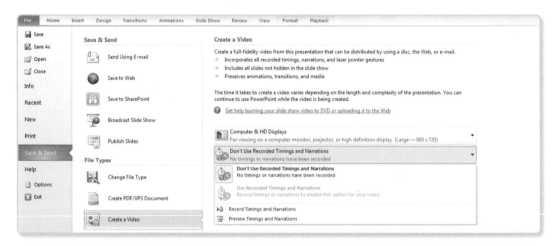

Above: Picture 2: Within the Create a Video options you can alter the default settings concerning timings and narration.

4. From the timings and narrations menu you can also preview your recording or make a new one before you create the video.

5. Once you're happy with your settings, click on Create Video. You'll need to pick a name and save destination (My Documents, Desktop, etc.), and then hit Save.

Hot Tip

If you're watching the video on a Mac, download the VLC video player, which will embrace the Microsoft format on your Apple machine.

6. Depending on the file size, it'll take a few minutes to export the video, which will be saved as a Windows Media Video (.wmv) file (this means you'll need Windows Media Player to play it).

How to Create a Video on a Mac

As we mentioned above, the method of creating a video differs only slightly to using a PC:

1. On a Mac, you need to select File and then Save as Movie. Select Movie Options from the pop-up Save Window to tailor the settings as follows (*see* Picture 1):

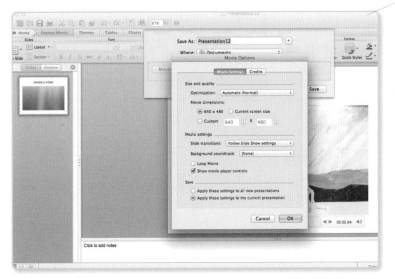

Above: Picture 1: Mac users must select File > Save as Movie. You can then tailor your settings from the pop-up Save Window summoned by Movie Options.

- **Size and Quality:** Here you can optimize the presentation for Quality, Size, Smooth Playback or Automatic, while also selecting the dimensions of your move. The default is 640 x 480: a medium quality setting, ideal for viewing online or burning to DVD.

Hot Tip

If you plan to export your presentation as a video from the get-go, you might prefer to design the slides in the widescreen (16:9) aspect ration (*see* page 49). This will ensure that the slide show fills the screen without any unsightly black borders.

- **Media Settings:** Here you can select whether to include your slide transitions, whether to loop the video (ideal if it's playing at an exhibit), whether to show movie player controls *and* whether to add a soundtrack. That's right: you can import any song from your computer as a soundtrack to your presentation.

- **Credits:** If you so desire, you can add director, producer, performers listings and more, but these won't appear within your exported video.

2. Once you're happy with the settings, you can choose a file name and save destination, and hit Save to store it on your Mac. The movie will be saved as a .mov file, which will open on your computer in the QuickTime program.

Adding Narration to a Soundtrack on Mac

For some reason, unbeknownst to most mere mortals outside of Microsoft HQ, video versions of your presentation in PowerPoint for Mac *do not* include the soundtrack you've recorded.

There are a couple of ways around this, but they are fiddly. After you've exported your video file, open it within the iMovie video editing software that came with your Mac. Here you can add a new soundtrack to your video by recording and speaking as the slides progress. Use the Help Menus within iMovie for more detailed instructions.

Another method is to record the narrations separately using a free third-party program like Audacity (download it from audacity.sourceforge.net).

Uploading Your Video to the Internet

The final step in the video creation process is the most important. In order to deliver it to the masses, so they can access your beautiful slide show on-demand, you'll need to upload it to the internet. We'd suggest the most popular solution on the planet: YouTube. Uploading is criminally simple, but here are the key steps.

- Go to www.youtube.com and log in (you'll need a free Google account or Gmail address).

- Hit the Upload button at the top right of the YouTube homepage.

- On the next screen, hit the Select from your computer menu and pick your video, which will then start the upload.

- While the video is uploading you can type in a title, write a description and choose whether you want to make it available to the public, make it available to those with the link, or keep it private.

- Once the upload is complete, copy the link to the video and send it to your students, work colleagues, family members or whomever you'd like.

Above: Uploading your video to YouTube is simple if you stick the steps above.

SLIDE LIBRARIES

PowerPoint contains plenty of tools to cut down on the amount of work you have to do. Slide Masters (*see* page 129) allow you add common objects to all slides, while you can easily duplicate slides when minimal changes are required. Another way, which we've not yet covered, is to pull them in from other presentations. This is perfect if you've created a host of stunningly designed presentation slides that you'd like to use over and over again for new presentations, or those where few changes are required.

IMPORTING SLIDES

1. When selecting a New Slide from the home tab, hit Reuse Slides from the very bottom of the drop-down menu (it's called Insert Slide from Other Presentation on Mac). This will launch the pane you'll see to the right of the screen below (it's all done from a pop-up window on Mac).

2. Click the Insert Slide From option on PC (it's already selected on Mac), choose the presentation from which you'd like to borrow a slide and then click Open.

Above: You can insert slides by using the Reuse Slides button from the New Slide drop-down menu.

3. This will display the thumbnail images of slides from that presentation within the Reuse pane (pop-up window on Mac). Click them to automatically insert the slide within your current presentation (on a Mac you can select multiple slides and then hit Insert or Insert All).

4. All features of the imported slide will remain the same.

Using Slide Libraries

This is an option that will not be available to the vast majority of PowerPoint users as it requires your school or office to be signed up with Microsoft SharePoint (*see* page 196) and requires Microsoft PowerPoint Professional Plus (there's no way we're forking out for that!) but it's a really handy tool nonetheless.

SharePoint allows multiple users access to a library of PowerPoint slides created by multiple people. It's perfect if your team creates a lot of PowerPoint presentations where uniform information and design are required. If you know this functionality is already set up in your office you can easily publish slides to SharePoint or, in turn, grab from the library to use in your own presentations.

↪ **To publish slides to SharePoint (PC only):** Hit File to enter Backstage View, select Save & Send and then click Publish Slides. Then select the slides you'd like to publish, enter the URL for the library (you'll need to grab this from your system administrator, i.e. call the IT guy!) and hit Publish.

↪ **To import a slide from SharePoint (PC only):** From the Reuse Slides pane (*see* screenshot on page 218) hit the Browse button and select Browse Slide Library; this will give you options from the shared library. Then to select the presentation use the same methods explained in the Reuse Slides section on the previous page.

Macros

Macros are mini programs written by users to help perform regular, yet time-consuming, tasks within Microsoft Office programs such as PowerPoint (this feature lives within the Tools menu on Mac and the View tab on PC). The idea is that a number of actions that usually take several steps can instead be performed in one keyboard short cut. There's little reason for us to investigate them at the moment, but if you'd like to learn more head to www.office.com and search for Macros in the support pages.

POWERPOINT PROJECTS

PROJECT 1:
RE-CREATING HISTORY FOR TEACHERS AND STUDENTS

PowerPoint can be a great classroom tool and here we'll show you how to create a simple history-based presentation. Bulleted lists can point out the key facts and SmartArt can relay a sequence of events, while audio and YouTube clips furnish the presentation with entertaining, interesting content from further sources. Here's a step-by-step guide, using PowerPoint 2010 for PC, to creating a slide show we'll call 'The Real King's Speech'.

1. Open PowerPoint (Start > All Programs > Microsoft Office > PowerPoint) and begin a Blank Presentation (Control+N). Hit the Design tab in the Ribbon to select a theme from the drop-down menu.

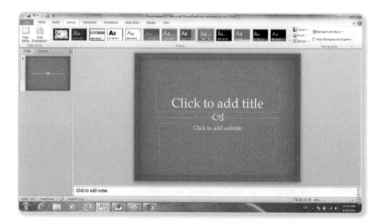

Step 1: Choose a design that will reflect the theme of your presentation.

This particularly regal presentation would be best served by the Hardcover theme, which should now adorn the first slide.

2. Choose a title and subtitle (try to keep both within two lines to ensure they are neat and highly visible). Click within the pre-set boxes and start to type.

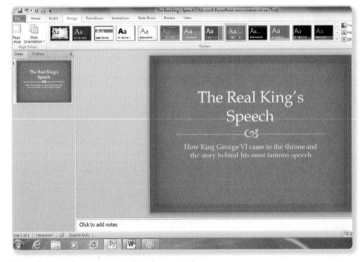

Step 2: Try to fit your text within the preset boxes.

3. Click Control+M to add a new slide (repeat this step whenever adding a new slide). By default, this will add a Title and Content placeholder slide. Give the slide a title and then click within the content placeholder. After every piece of text information, hit the Enter key to create a new bullet point.

4. Add a video from YouTube to break up the text-based slides. Using a new slide, hit Layout from the Home tab and select the Title Only option. Select the Insert tab, click the video icon and select Video from Web Site.

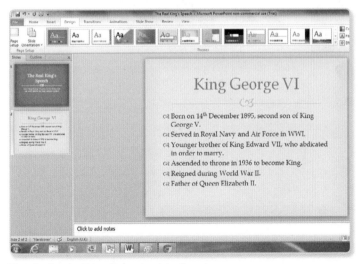

Step 3: : Pressing Enter after each point will create a regally-themed bullet point.

Step 5: The long embed code will link your slide to the video of your choice.

Step 6: The cursor on your screen allows you to place the video wherever you like on your slide.

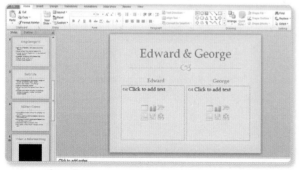

Step 7: Encourage feedback from the class by asking for comparisons between the brothers.

5. Head to www.youtube.com and find your clip. Copy the embed code (*see* page 153 for instructions) and paste that into the dialogue box open on your slide.

6. Press OK. Resize the video by dragging on the corners and position it where you need it on the slide by picking up the object with your cursor and moving it into place.

7. On a new slide, select the Comparison layout. Click on the relevant placeholder, select the Insert Image icon, choose the pictures from the folder where they are saved on your computer and click Insert. In this case, feature pictures of Edward VII and George VI, and call upon the class to discuss the difference between the two men.

8. Adding further text-based slides at this point would be acceptable without risking information overload but be careful of running too many text-only slides in a row. Add the new Title and Content slide, and add the information as you did in Step 3. As this particular slide represents

a timeline of information, we can convert text to a SmartArt diagram. Once you've highlighted the bulleted list (Control+A selects all text), right-click, hit Convert to SmartArt and select the Staggered diagram from the Process category within the More SmartArt Graphics menu.

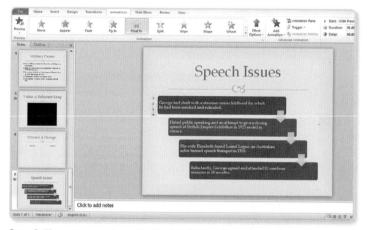

Step 9: The points seen here will arrive one by one if you choose Float In from the Animations tab.

9. Select the SmartArt diagram and then click the Animations tab. Choose the Float In animation and then choose One by One from Effect Options drop-down menu. This will ensure the points arrive on screen at your command.

10. In order to add an end-of-slide show quiz for the class, use one bullet for each question and a secondary paragraph for the answer.

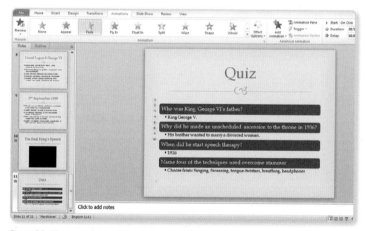

Step 10: To retain the audience's attention, have the answers to your end-of-show quiz float in via the Animations tab.

To add a secondary paragraph, press the Tab key on the keyboard to indent it underneath the previous point. Then follow the instructions listed in Step 9 to ensure the question and then the answers appear in stages using Animations.

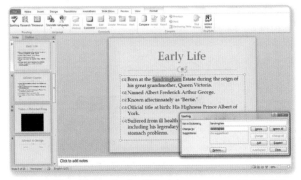

Step 11: Use the Spell Check to ensure your presentation does not look slap-dash and amateur.

Step 13: Remember to print out your prompt notes, and also handouts for your classmates.

11. Select the Spelling tool from within the Review tab. You can accept or ignore suggested corrections and add words to the dictionary. Once the check is done, you'll see a message that says: 'The spelling check is complete'.

12. Revisit the slides and add Transitions. Select the slide you want to move to (not from) and click the Transitions tab from the Ribbon. Click on the transition of your choice (e.g. Split, Push, Wipe) and you'll see an instant preview on screen. Use the Timing pane to control how long a transition lasts and whether a sound is played. Hit the Apply To All button to add your transitions to every slide.

13. Add notes to help deliver the presentation and ensure all talking points are covered. Enter the Notes tab at the bottom of each slide and type the information you'd like to recall. To print Notes Pages click Control+P and then select Notes Pages from the Print Layout menu (from this menu, you can also print handouts).

14. Connect to the external monitor (*see* page 73) and press the F5 key to begin your presentation. From the Slide Show tab select Presenter View (*see* page 83). Move between slides or bullet points with the up/down arrows (for a full list of in-presentation tools *see* pages 81–82). When the show is over, click the Escape key.

PROJECT 2: TEACHING A FILM-MAKING CLASS

Traditionally, in order to teach a film class, a teacher would need a whiteboard (or blackboard), printed handouts and a DVD player – at least. This case study is an example of how PowerPoint can encapsulate multiple classroom tools to produce an interactive, all-in-one solution. Designed using PowerPoint 2011 for Mac, this is a slide show about basic film-making vocabulary and is illustrated by text, photos and videos.

1. Open PowerPoint by clicking the P icon within the Dock on your Mac. If PowerPoint doesn't appear within the Dock, press the Command+Space keyboard short cut to summon Spotlight and start typing PowerPoint. When the program appears in the list, click it to open.

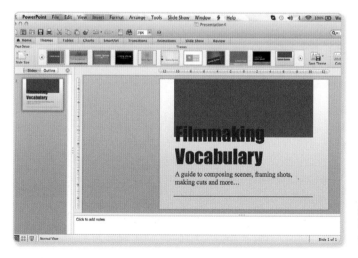

2. From the PowerPoint Presentation Gallery, select All Themes and choose one by selecting and clicking Choose. We've chosen the Newsprint theme.

Step 2: The Newsprint Theme looks extremely effective for this subject matter.

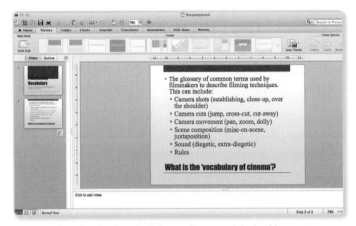

Step 3: After the title slide, your first main slide should summarize what the presentation will cover.

Step 6: Adding a shadow to your text boxes is a simple but effective method of adding interest to a slide.

3. Add a title and subtitle to the Title slide. Next, add a New Slide, by clicking that button within the Home tab. Create a text-based slide that embellishes upon your title by adding bullet points that summarize the topics to be covered during the class.

4. In order to start a new section, add a New Slide and then hit Create New Section from the Home tab; this will position a section between the two slides. Type a name for the section (we've called it 'Camera Shots'). Here you could ask the class to participate by naming shots they're familiar with before delving into detail on the next slide.

5. Add a New Slide and add text to the Title placeholder. Next, add a series of images to showcase a long shot, medium shot and close-up. In order to showcase each shot style, use the same photo but cropped (*see* page 141) differently.

6. Draw text boxes next to the thumbnail images (Home > Text > Text Box). Place the cursor

within each box and type descriptions of the shots by the photos. Add some style to the text boxes by selecting the Format pane and adding a Shape Style. Then hit Shape Effects and add some shadow or reflection.

7. Hit Command+D to create a Duplicate Slide, which will appear directly underneath. This will create a carbon copy, allowing you simply to replace the information rather than redesigning from scratch. In this slide you could add related terms, such as over-the-shoulder, crane, high angle, overhead, etc.

8. On the next New Slide, insert a pre-prepared video clip from your computer (Home > Insert > Media > Movie From File) which showcases each of the shots mentioned. Ask the class to point out the long, medium and close-up shots as they happen. Select the Format Movie tab, hit Playback Options and select Full Screen.

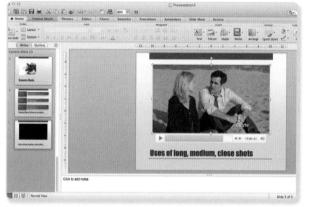

9. Repeat Step 4. Call the new section 'Camera Cuts'.

Step 8: Insert your video-clip and position it into the centre of the slide.

10. Design the new section (and subsequent sections) in the same way. Remember you can copy and paste slides to save design time and retain consistency. Just right-click the appropriate slide and hit Copy; then right-click again underneath the last slide in the show and press Paste. For illustrating Camera Cuts, replace the thumbnail images with videos from your computer.

11. For the section entitled *Mise en scène* (meaning 'what's in the frame') you could add a class exercise. Use a slide of bullet points to explain the definition of the term.

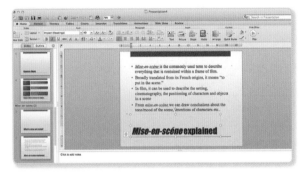

Step 11: Bulleted lists are a good way to prompt discussion.

Step 12: A quiz-based video clip should guarantee your audience sits up and takes notice: after all, the purpose of a presentation is to teach them something!

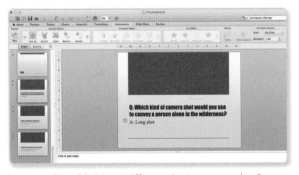

Step 14: Entrance Effect on the Animations tab will mean that you control when the answer appears.

12. Next, add a New Slide containing a video of a famous film scene from your computer (any scene from Martin Scorsese's *Taxi Driver* should work!). Use the text formatting tools to add emphasis to the keywords in the title. Show the video and then give the class five minutes to write down observations on the *mise en scène* employed by the film-maker and how it reflects upon the intended tone and meaning of the scene.

13. At the end of the video you could also add a quiz to test what the class gleaned from the presentation. Add a new section and call it 'Quiz'.

14. Add a New Slide and apply the Title Slide layout. Click inside the title placeholder and type in the question (use text formatting tools such as the Decrease Font Size in the Home tab to ensure it fits neatly). Add the answer in the subtitle, select the text and add an Entrance Effect from the Animations tab to ensure that the answer only appears when you're ready. Repeat this step for each question.

15. Save the presentation (Command+S).

16. In order to save the presentation online, where it can be accessed by colleagues and absent students, select File > Share > Save To SkyDrive. Insert Windows ID login details and select Save. If the presentation contains video it may take a while (for full details on sharing via SkyDrive, *see* page 41).

17. Spellcheck your slide show for errors (Tools > Spelling).

18. Use the Notes tab on each slide to add text-based reminders of the talking points you'd like to touch upon when discussing the contents of the presentation. This way, you won't forget anything.

19. Connect your laptop or computer to the in-class projector or external monitor using a HDMI or VGA cable (depending on the newness of your equipment) and use the display's remote control to select the correct input.

20. Select the Slide Show tab and select Presenter View. This showcases the current slide, next slide, slide notes and how long the slide show has been running. It'll also display the time of day to help ensure you don't overrun. Use the keyboard and mouse tools outlined in Chapter two (see pages 81–82) to deliver the slide show.

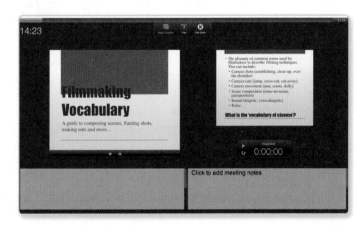

Step 20: Presenter View will give you a behind-the-scenes look at your presentation, including how much time you've taken to deliver it.

PROJECT 3:
THE FAMILY PHOTO ALBUM

PowerPoint allows excitable dads the world over to finally ditch the photo slide show carousel and create attractive photo slide shows in double-quick time for the whole family to ~~endure~~, sorry, enjoy. In this case study, we'll create an album from a template using PowerPoint 2011 for Mac.

1. Open PowerPoint from the P icon in the Dock. This will present the PowerPoint Presentation Gallery. Select Contemporary Photo Album from Templates > Presentations and click Choose.

Step 1: The Templates menu includes different layouts that are suitable for many projects, including Quiz Shows and Employee Training manuals.

2. On the Title slide, click the Sunflower photo and press delete to free up the placeholder. Then click Insert Picture from the Home tab and select from Photo Browser. Find the picture you'd like to use as a cover and drag it to the placeholder.

3. Templates feature full slide designs, but you can still select a theme from the tab to change the colour and font scheme. Here we've selected Advantage from the Theme tab.

4. Add a title and subtitle into the placeholders by clicking within them and typing. You'll see that the subtitle features a vertical text layout.

5. Templates feature a pre-set number of slides, and this template has six. Select the next slide in Slide View. If you're happy with the layout, repeat steps 2 and 4 to add a photo and text. To change it, select Layout in the Home tab to choose from various combinations of photo and caption boxes.

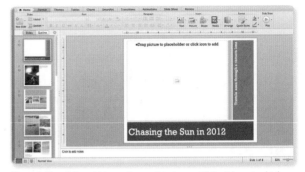

Step 4: The slides within each template have a default layout which can be changed by going to Home tab > Layout.

6. Use the Crop tools that appear when inserting a picture to ensure that the part of the photo you wish to highlight is situated within the frame. Press Crop to summon the resizing tools and drag the markers to increase or decrease size. Then click the photo and drag it into the correct position within the frame.

Step 6: Get it just how you want it! Pressing Crop will bring up resizing tools so you can do just that.

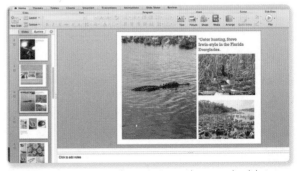

7. All slides are fully customizable so you're not limited to adding photos to placeholders. You can insert a picture anywhere onto a slide (Home > Insert > Picture > From File) and then resize and crop to your specifications.

Step 7: You can arrange and rearrange your photos on the slide just as you can in a traditional photo album.

Step 8: The Picture Format tab contains features and effects that will give your PowerPoint album a professional touch.

Step 9: To see how this photo looks as a full slide, look at the bottom of the left-hand column of this screenshot.

Step 10: Unlike traditional photo albums, your PowerPoint album can feature video alongside the photographs.

8. The full range of picture styles and format tools are available. You can add soft edges, frames and effects from the Picture Format tab, as you can see left.

9. To add a full slide photo, right-click a slide, select Layout and then Blank. Insert the photo and use the Crop tool (see Step 6) to increase the size without altering the aspect ratio of the picture. If you'd like to add a caption use Insert > Text. Draw the text box and type your caption; select the drop-down font colour tools to ensure it doesn't clash with your photo.

10: In order to add a video, insert a Title and Content slide, and select the Video icon from the placeholder. Select the video from your computer and it will be inserted into the slide. In the Format Movie tab select Poster Frame to add an image that shows before you play the video.

11. The Contemporary Photo Album template only has six slides. Add more with the New Slide button (along with your choice of layout) in the Home tab and continue adding slides and photos until you've completed the album.

12. Hit Slide Sorter View in the Status Bar and drag each slide into your preferred position if you'd like to rearrange photos.

13. Save your presentation (Command+S).

14. Hook your laptop up to your HDTV using a HDMI or VGA cable. Select the corresponding Input on your TV set and deliver the presentation from the Slide Show tab (use the mouse/keyboard tools set out on pages 81–82).

15. If you're connecting with someone further afield why not broadcast the presentation online? That way anyone in the world with access to a web browser can tune in.

Step 12: Using the Slide Sorter View, it's easy to rearrange your slides before you show the album to your family

Step 17: Family abroad? Let them share the experience by broadcasting your album online.

16. Before you broadcast, you may like to record a narration track. Select the Slide Show tab, hit Record Slide Show and talk about each slide (for more instructions see page 209). The track is recorded by your computer's internal microphone. Press Escape when complete and ensure Use Narrations is ticked in the Set Up pane.

17. Hit Broadcast Show, click Connect and then enter your Windows ID (Hotmail, etc.). Once PowerPoint has prepared the presentation, copy the on-screen link and send it to your absent friend/family members via email. When you know they've tuned in, press Play Slide Show.

PROJECT 4:
THE FAMILY DIET AND FITNESS REGIME

Believe it or not, there are endless uses for PowerPoint in the home beyond the traditional family photo album. This case study will tackle the unenviable task of convincing the troops that less treats and more exercise is actually a good idea. It will feature the foods that have to go, make the alternatives seem exciting and outline a regime for the new, healthier era. This presentation is designed using PowerPoint 2010 for PC.

1. Open PowerPoint. Click Start > All Programs > Microsoft Office and click PowerPoint. This will bring up a new Blank Presentation, featuring a single Title Slide. Select the Design tab in the Ribbon and choose a theme from the drop-down menu in the centre of the pane. The Civic theme feels clean and sleek.

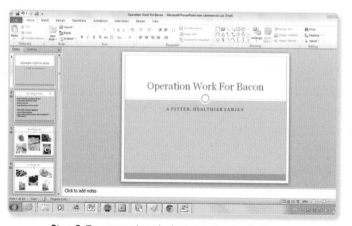

Step 2: Type your title and subtitle into the placeholders.

2. Add a title and subtitle to your slide by clicking within each of the respective placeholders and typing. This presentation is called 'Operation Work for Bacon: A Fitter, Healthier Family'.

3. Add an image to the Title Slide. Select the Insert tab and hit the Clip Art button. Type 'Fruit' into the search bar and press Enter. From the search results click the image of your choice and it will appear on the slide. In order to tailor the image perfectly, press Crop in the Picture Format Tools and pull in the margins to reflect the preferred size. Then drag the picture itself to the correct position within the margins. Press the Crop button again when happy.

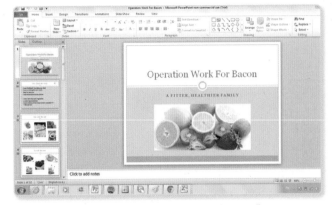

Step 3: You can add an image from PowerPoint's Clip Art gallery, or from elsewhere on your computer.

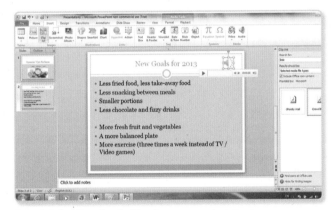

Step 4: Follow Step 4 and add audio to your presentation to lighten the mood and get your audience's attention.

4. Add a New Slide (Control+M) to create a bullet-pointed list of goals. As this news isn't likely to be received well, you can add an audio clip to the slide. Clip Art features a Crowd Booing sound effect. Hit the Insert tab and select Audio and then Clip Art Audio. Search for 'Boo' and then click to add the .wav file to the slide. Select the Audio Playback tab and then Start from Audio Options. Select Automatically so that the sound plays when the slide appears.

5. Add a New Slide (Control+M). Right-click it in the Slide Sorter View and select Layout. Change to Title Only. Use this slide to add pictures (see Step 3) of foods that will be eliminated.

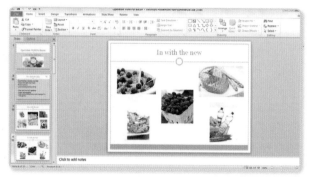

Step 6: Use the tips you learned in Chapter 3 to add Animations to your presentation.

Add an Exit Effect animation for each individual image to make them disappear from the slide (click the Image, then Animations, Exit Effects, Fade) with each click of the mouse.

6. Repeat this on the next slide, in reverse order, but use healthier food pictures from Clip Art. Once the images have been positioned, add an Entrance Effect to each one from the Animations tab. They will appear on screen with each click.

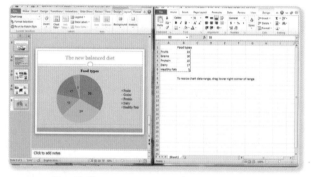

Step 7: If you want to insert a chart to your presentation, Excel and PowerPoint work together to do it for you.

7. In order to add a pie chart to showcase a balanced diet, create a new slide and use the Chart icon within the placeholder to select Pie. Excel should now launch next to PowerPoint. Add your percentage figures to the Excel datasheet and they'll translate to the chart automatically.

8. On the next slide, insert a video from YouTube to showcase alternatives to the current meals. Select Insert > Video > Video from Web Site. Copy and paste the YouTube embed code as explained on page 153 to insert the clip.

9. To illustrate the new fitness regime, add a new slide and click the Table icon from the placeholder. Select eight rows and five columns (enough for the seven days and four family members) and fill in the activities for each person to correspond with the day of the week.

10. Add a new slide with the Section Header layout to begin work on the Rewards section.

11. Create a bullet-pointed list of incentives on a new slide. Use Animations to ensure each point appears one at a time on the screen.

12. On the final slide ('The Ultimate Incentive') add a teaser link to the main reward. Highlight the 'Click here' portion of the text, hit the Insert tab, press Hyperlink (see page 190) and copy the URL from a website into the address box of the pop-up window (this could reveal a holiday destination like Disney World) and select OK. Remember that the link will only work in Slide Show mode.

13. As you're delivering the presentation to a small family unit, have them gather round the screen. Press F5 on the keyboard to enter Presentation Mode and use the mouse/keyboard tools explained on pages 81–82 to control the presentation. Press Escape when the presentation is complete.

Step 8: Why not add a video for some extra inspiration? It's easy to do, and you could insert a different clip every week.

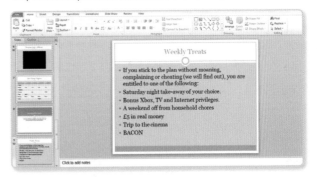

Step 11: Add Animations to make the items on your list appear one by one, heightening the tension before the final point is revealed!

Step 12: Use what you learned in Chapter five about Hyperlinks to add one to your slideshow.

PROJECT 5: THE OFFICE PITCH

When you're building a case for change, PowerPoint can be one of the most powerful tools you can harness. You can use a slide show packed with charts, figures, videos and facts to convince your colleagues that your way is the right way. In this case study, we're convincing the company that iPhones should replace BlackBerry phones. This presentation is built using PowerPoint for Mac 2011.

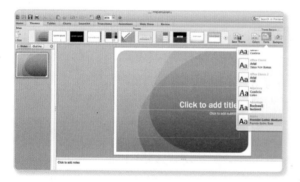

Step 2: Play around with the font pairings to try out different combinations (Themes tab > Theme Options > Fonts).

1. Select the PowerPoint icon from the Dock on your Mac computer to open the software. Cancel the PowerPoint Gallery view to start a new Blank Presentation.

2. Hit the Themes tab and select a design. We've selected Revolution, as it is formal yet attractive. To select a different font pairing, choose Fonts from the Theme Options pane of the Themes tab. We borrowed the fonts from the Angles theme: Franklin Gothic Medium and Franklin Gothic Book.

3. Click your mouse within the placeholders and begin typing text. We've called the slideshow 'iPhone vs BlackBerry' with the subtitle 'Time for a change?'

4. Insert photos of the BlackBerry and iPhone onto the Title page using the Picture from File option within the Home tab. Once they're both on screen, use the Remove Background

tool in the Picture Format tab (*see* page 142 for detailed instructions). Resize and reposition according to your preference.

5. In order to make the iPhone fly in and the BlackBerry fly out, select the iPhone image, hit the Animations tab and click 'Fly In' from the Entrance Effects pane. In the Animation Options pane, select Effect Options and choose From Left; also, increase the Duration from 0.5 second to 1 second.

Step 4: By using the Remove Background option in the Picture Format tab, you can get rid of any unwanted items or areas from your photographs.

6. Repeat this on the BlackBerry but select Fly Out from the Exit Effects and From Right from the Effect Options menu. Hit the Reorder button to summon the Custom Animation menu. Increase the delay to 2 seconds and, from the same menu, click Start and hit After Previous rather than On Click. Select the Preview button to see how it looks

7. Hit New Slide from the Home tab within the Ribbon. We've typed 'The Proposal' into the Title box, but the font feels too small so we've selected the text (Command+A) and used the Increase Font Size button in the Home tab to bump up the font.

8. Type in the proposal points and press Enter after each one to create a new bullet point. Hit the Animations tab, select all text (Command+A) and add Blinds from the Entrance Effects pane. This will ensure that each point arrives one at a time when presenting. Repeat this process for all additional text-based slides.

Step 6: Use the options given within the Entrance and Exit Effects panes to create some dramatic moments in your presentation.

Step 9: Using the tools within the Movie Options pane, you can make your video clip start automatically when you reach that particular slide.

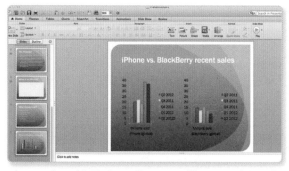

Step 10: The Insert Chart icon will bring up a choice of charts that you can add to your presentation.

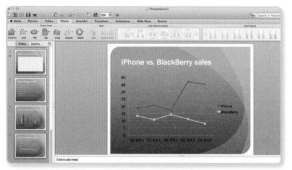

Step 11: To transform bar charts into a line graph, choose Line from the chart menu and combine your data in Excel.

9. On a new slide, click the Video icon within the content placeholder and select the file on your computer. To make the clip start automatically when the slide appears, click Start and select Automatically from the Movie Options pane.

10. On a new slide, select the Two Content layout option from the Home tab. In each content placeholder select the Insert Chart icon and choose from the Bar Chart options. This will summon Microsoft Excel with a default datasheet that will populate your chart. Replace the data in Excel with the figures and categories of your choice. Changes will be reflected in the on-screen charts. When complete, there will be charts depicting recent iPhone and BlackBerry sales.

11. In order to drive the point home, turn the data from both charts into a single line graph. This time select Line from the chart menu and then combine the data from before into one Excel datasheet. Make sure you use Switch Plots in the Chart Layout tab to ensure it looks right. Categories should appear in the vertical axis while sales numbers appear in the vertical axis.

12. Add a 'voice' from employees. Select the SmartArt tab from the Ribbon. Hit the List pane and select Vertical Picture Accent. Click on the picture placeholder and insert photos of the spokespeople. Use the Crop tools in Picture Format to ensure faces appear within the frame. You can fill the speech boxes with soundbite text by clicking within them and typing.

13. To change the look and feel, select SmartArt > Shape Styles. The screenshot to the right showcases the white outline that has been added for emphasis. Next, we selected Right to Left from the Edit SmartArt pane to switch thumbnail pictures to the other side of the text. Lastly, we used the Align tool to place the SmartArt at the left of the slide, to match the headline.

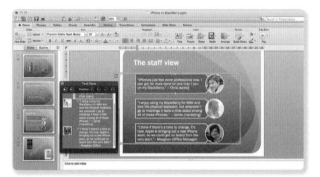

Step 13: Try the various options within SmartArt to give your presentation a professional edge.

14. Add a new Blank Side (New Slide > Layout > Blank). Draw a text box and add the title 'Questions'. Select the text and use Text Effects from the Format tab to give the title more style. Next, copy the pictures from the Title slide (Command+C) and paste into the new slide (Command+P) for design continuity.

15. Save your presentation (File > Save or Command+S).

16. Before delivering the presentation, use the spellcheck tool (Tools > Spelling) to check for authority-undermining typing errors. Practise the presentation using the Play Presentation tool in the Slide Show tab.

17. Hook up to a HDTV or projector in your office conference room and select Presenter View from the Slide Show tab. Deliver your presentation using all of the tools mentioned back in Chapter two (*see* pages 81–82).

PROJECT 6:
INITIATING A NEW POLICY

PowerPoint can be the HR professional's or office manager's best friend for training new employees and educating the current crop about changes in policy. The following case study – an employee guide to the advantages and potential pitfalls of using social media – has been designed using PowerPoint 2010 for PC.

1. Open PowerPoint and start a new Blank Presentation by pressing Control+N. Select the Design tab and choose a theme for your presentation. We have selected the Concourse design.

2. Add a title and a subtitle to your presentation. We've chosen 'Using Social Media', with the subtitle 'The do's and don'ts of safe social networking'.

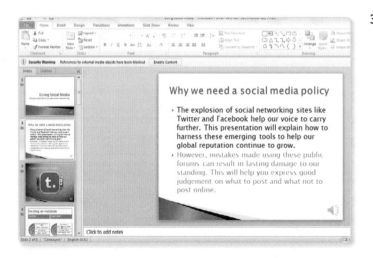

3. Add a new slide (Control+M). In this introductory slide, place your cursor within the content placeholder and type the statements to outline the purpose of the presentation, offering a framework for the positive and negative aspects of social media.

    Step 3: The introductory slide should offer a snapshot of what the presentation will cover.

4. Add a new Title Only slide to the presentation from the Home tab. To introduce the different types of social media, insert a picture of that company's logo from the Insert tab. Once the image is added, select the Animations tab and add an Entrance Effect (Float In) and an Exit Effect (Float Out).

5. Continue to add the remaining logos, adding the Animations as you do so. Eventually, all of the logos will appear to be piled on top of each other in the centre of the slide, but fret not; in Presentation Mode, they'll float in and float out one at a time, allowing you to speak about them individually. To reorder the images click the Selection Pane from the Picture Tools Format menu and use the up/down Re-order arrows.

6. On a New Slide select the Comparison layout to write Do Post/Don't Post comparison lists. Once you've completed both bullet-pointed lists, select the text within each, right-click and choose Convert to SmartArt. Here we've selected the Target List diagram.

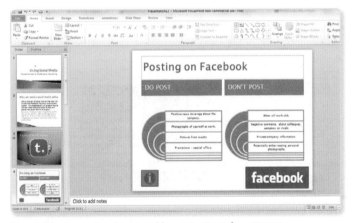

Step 6: The Comparison layout enables contrasting information to be included side by side, offering two differing opinions.

7. On the same slide, select Shapes from the Insert tab. Scroll all the way down to Action Buttons and choose the Information box. Draw it in the bottom corner of the slide; this will summon the Action Settings menu. From Hyperlink to select the URL option and then copy the web address for a 'Social Media Disasters' article. This can be clicked from the presentation.

8. Add a new Title and Content slide from the Home tab and write a bulleted list on responsible tweeting tips within the content placeholder. To avoid the risk of information overload,

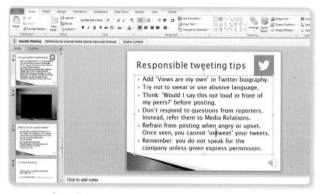

Step 8: You can make the bullets 'fly' onto the slide, rather like a tweet arriving perhaps, using the options given within the Animations tab.

Step 9: Make use of the myriad videos on sharing websites to add a voice of authority to your presentation.

try to keep the number of bullet points at six or less. From the Animations tab, add the effects of your choice and customize them using Effect Options. You could repeat this step to explain policy on other networks (e.g. LinkedIn), YouTube and personal blogs.

9. Add a new Title Only slide. Type in your title and then select the Insert tab. Click Video and then Video from Web Site. Head to www.youtube.com and find the video of your choosing. Copy the embed code using the instructions on page 153 and paste it into the dialogue box back within the PowerPoint Window. This video will outline the argument before advancing to the next bullet-pointed slide: 'When to Use Social Media'.

10. As we're going to be emailing this presentation to everyone in the company, as well as presenting it to an audience, insert a 'Further Reading' slide, complete with links to the full Social Media Policy and an email address so you can field questions. To add the hyperlinks, highlight the relevant piece of text, click Insert and then Hyperlink, and copy the website URL and email address into the relevant boxes within the pop-up window.

11. Save (Control+S) and spellcheck (Review > Spelling) your presentation.

12. Select the Transitions tab and choose the drop-down arrow. Pick from one of the Dynamic Content options (such as Rotate or Pan) and click Apply To All.

13. Enter the Backstage View (File tab). From the Info menu select Compress Media to optimize the file size for sharing. Select the Low Quality option to enable sharing via email attachment.

Step 13: Compressing your presentation will make it suitable for sending via email.

14. From the same page select Prepare for Sharing. The Compatibility Checker will ensure that everything you've included will be viewable in earlier versions of PowerPoint.

15. Hit Save & Send in the Backstage View and select Send Using Email. Click the Send as Attachment option. This will launch your email client (Outlook) with the attached presentation sitting within a new blank email.

Step 16: The Handouts option within Print > Print Layout will include lines next to each slide on which the audience can make notes.

16. In order to prepare for your presentation to an audience, select the Print option. From the Print Layout menu select Handouts (3 slides per page), add the number of copies and select the Print button.

17. Deliver your presentation using the tools outlined in Chapter two (*see* page 81).

JARGON BUSTER

Action Button
A button where clicking or hovering the mouse over it triggers an Action, such as linking to a website or moving to the next slide.

Align
Control how text or an object appears within a slide, horizontally and vertically (e.g. hugging the left or right, or centre, top or bottom).

Animation
Effects that control how objects behave when entering and leaving a presentation (e.g. Fly, Fade, Float).

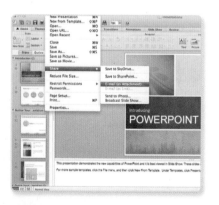

Arrange
Control the order in which objects appear within the slide by bringing them forward or sending them backwards.

Aspect Ratio
The height and width of slides relative to each other (e.g. 4:3 or 16:9).

AutoCorrect
When PowerPoint assumes you've made an error and corrects it.

AutoFormat
Makes automatic formatting changes to your presentation (e.g. 1/2 becomes ½).

Axis
The horizontal and vertical lines on which data is plotted (e.g. days of the week, ice cream sold).

Background Style
Controls the colours, shading, patterns or images that appear behind the objects on your slides.

Backstage View
Microsoft's pet name for the File tab, which controls most of the essential 'behind the scenes' functionality, such as saving, printing, etc.

Browser
A tool for viewing internet-based content (e.g. Internet Explorer, Firefox, Chrome).

Bullet
A text character that helps to arrange words in listed form.

Clip Art
Images, videos, illustrations and audio built into the PowerPoint software, which can easily be added to slides.

Clipboard
Stores information that users copy or cut from content placeholders or slides.

Content Placeholder
A design pre-set, which allows you to add objects like text, images, video and charts to a slide.

Crop
Trimming the size of an image.

Cursor
The icon that appears on the screen representing your mouse pointer.

Datasheet
The collection of figures from which a table or chart is created.

Default Settings
The pre-set actions that occur when accessing features within PowerPoint.

Demote
The action of moving a sentence or paragraph down one level within a list (the opposite of promote).

Drag
Selecting an object with your mouse, holding down the mouse button and pulling it to a new location.

Effects
Formatting tools that allow shadows, reflections, rotations and more.

Equations
A collection of numbers and symbols, usually representing a mathematical formula.

Excel
Microsoft Office spreadsheet program, useful in PowerPoint for creating charts.

Fill
The colour information within a shape. 'No fill' means that there's a clear background.

Fonts
The collective term for the different text styles.

Footers
Information that resides at the bottom of a slide (i.e. date, title, name).

Formatting
Altering the size, colour and style of an object in PowerPoint.

Grayscale
A slide, print-out or presentation which only features shades of grey.

Handout
A printed document which showcases each slide from your presentation.

Header

Text information that appears at the top of one or all slides (usually features the title or date).

Hyperlink

A link to an object within a slide (e.g. a website, different presentation, next slide).

Justify

How text or an object sits within the placeholder. Text that is evenly spread across the text box, rather than aligned to the left, right or centre, is justified.

Landscape

A horizontally orientated slide, presentation or handout.

Layouts

The differing slide designs available within a presentation (e.g. Title and Content, Blank, Two Content).

Legend

A table featuring a colour-coded key to categories represented within a chart.

Macros

Mini programs that allow users to repeat routine tasks automatically.

Master

A Master controls all of the default formatting information for slides, handouts and notes. It can be customized, adjusted, added to and saved.

Merge

The process of combining two presentations to create one master document.

Motion Path

A custom animation feature, which allows an object to move across a pre-set path.

Object

Any item within PowerPoint (e.g. text box, photograph, shape, chart, table). Formatting and design tools can be applied to all objects.

Office Button

PowerPoint 2007 features a circular button in the top left side of the Window containing basic functionality like Open, New, Save, Print and Share.

Outline

Controls the colour of the text outline.

Pane

A vertical section of the PowerPoint Window (e.g. Slide View, Animation Pane, Current Slide View).

Portrait
A slide, handout or presentation with a vertical orientation.

Presentation
A collection of slides.

Promote
The action of moving a sentence or paragraph up one level within a list (the opposite of demote).

Quick Access Toolbar
Sitting above the Ribbon, it offers one-click access to a host of essential features.

Ribbon
The name for the PowerPoint user interface featuring tabs such as Home, Insert, Transitions.

Right-click
Hitting the button on the right side your mouse. On Mac computers this is achieved by hitting Control+Click or, on newer models, by clicking the mouse button with two fingers.

Series
Information that appears within a data or chart. A series represents one group of data results.

Shapes
Types of objects that can be drawn on to slides.

SmartArt
Text-based diagrams which can represent a relationship, flow or hierarchy of information.

Start Button
The Windows icon in the bottom left corner of the screen: access PowerPoint and other programs from here.

Tab
Subsections of a Window, such as each of the options within the Ribbon (Home, Insert, Slide Show, etc.).

Theme
A combination of design features used throughout a presentation.

Trackpad
The touch-sensitive centre section on a laptop computer that acts like a mouse.

Transition
The means of moving between slides (e.g. Dissolve, Push, Wipe, Split).

WordArt
A text design feature that includes a host of colours, fills, outlines and effects.

FURTHER READING

ECDL Advanced Syllabus 2.0 Module AM6 Presentation Using PowerPoint 2010, CiA Training, 2010.

Microsoft Official Academic Course: Microsoft PowerPoint 2010 MOS Exam 77-883, John Wiley & Sons, 2010.

Atkinson, Cliff, *Beyond Bullet Points 3rd Edition: Using Microsoft PowerPoint to Create Presentations That Inform, Motivate, and Inspire*, Microsoft Press, 2011.

Cox, Joyce and Lambert, Joan, *Microsoft PowerPoint 2010 Step By Step*, Microsoft Press, 2010.

Duarte, Nancy, *Resonate: Present Visual Stories That Transform Audiences*, John Wiley & Sons, 2010.

Duarte, Nancy, *slide:ology: The Art and Science of Creating Great Presentations*, O'Reilly Media, 2008.

Edney, Andrew, *PowerPoint 2007 in Easy Steps*, Computer Step, 2007.

Edney, Andrew, *PowerPoint 2010 in Easy Steps*, In Easy Steps Limited, 2010.

Gallo, Carmine, *The Presentation Secrets of Steve Jobs: How to Be Insanely Great in Front of Any Audience*, McGraw-Hill Professional, 2009.

Grover, Chris, *Office 2011 for Macintosh: The Missing Manual*, Pogue Press, 2010

Johnson, Steve, *Brilliant PowerPoint 2010: What You Need To Know and How You Do It*, Prentice Hall, 2010.

Kao, Wayne & Huang, Jeff, *Advanced Microsoft Office PowerPoint 2007: Insights and Advice From The Experts*, QUE, 2007.

LeVitus, Bob, *Office 2011 for Mac for Dummies*, John Wiley & Sons, 2011.

Lowe, Doug, *PowerPoint 2003 for Dummies*, John Wiley & Sons, 2003.

Lowe, Doug, *PowerPoint 2007 for Dummies*, John Wiley & Sons, 2007.

Lowe, Doug, *PowerPoint 2010 for Dummies*, John Wiley & Sons, 2010.

Reynolds, Garr, *Presentation Zen: Simply Ideas on Presentation Design and Delivery*, New Riders, 2011.

Wempen, Faithe, *PowerPoint 2003 Bible*, John Wiley & Sons, 2003.

Wempen, Faithe, *PowerPoint 2007 Bible*, John Wiley & Sons, 2007.

Wempen, Faithe, *PowerPoint 2010 Bible*, John Wiley & Sons, 2010.

WEBSITES

www.actden.com/pp/
PowerPoint in the classroom.

www.dummies.com/how-to/computers-
software/ms-office/powerpoint.html
The official online portal for the popular and
entertaining *For Dummies* series of books, including
a section on Microsoft Office and PowerPoint.

www.electricteacher.com/tutorial3.htm
Microsoft PowerPoint Tutorials.

www.microsoft.com/Education/en-
us/teachers/how-to/Pages/index.aspx
Microsoft Education's 'how to' pages.

www.microsoft.com/learning/en/us/
Exam.aspx?ID=77-883&Locale=en-us
Take an exam in PowerPoint 2010.

www.microsoft.com/office365
Office Online Services – hosted in the Cloud.

www.msofficeforums.com/powerpoint/
A community-based resource for all Office
products, including PowerPoint.

www.office.com
Get free trials of Microsoft Office, including
PowerPoint, and access the vast knowledge base.

www.powerpointstyles.com/
100% free PowerPoint templates
for personal use.

www.presentationload.com/powerpoint
Premium pay-to-download PowerPoint template
and slide designs.

www.presentationmagazine.com/
An online guide to making speeches and using
PowerPoint. There are also free-to-download
PowerPoint templates.

presentationsoft.about.com/od/
powerpoint101/a/begin_guide.htm
Beginner's Guide to PowerPoint 2010.

www.sharepoint.com
Learn more about this business-centric
collaboration tool.

slideshop.com/powerpoint-templates/
A PowerPoint resource store featuring a host
of templates, charts, shapes and diagrams.

www.skydrive.com
Microsoft's cloud-based storage solution.
Sign up for 25GB of free storage to share
and edit presentations online.

INDEX